Fodor's POCKET

munich

D0752674

fourth edition

Excerpted from Fodor's *Germany*

fodor's travel publications
new york • toronto • london • sydney • auckland
www.fodors.com

contents

maps

germany

DENMARK

100 miles

150 km

N

Rügen

Baltic Sea

Flensburg

Fehmarn

North Sea

Husum

Stralsund

Barth

Kiel

Rostock

Neustadt

Greifswald

Cuxhaven

Güstrow

Anklam

Caroliensiel

Lübeck

Wismar

Teterow

Neubrandenburg

Norden

Schwerin

Waren

Wilhelmshaven

Bremerhaven

Hamburg

Neustadt-Glewe

Neustrelitz

Emden

Ludwigslust

Pritzwalk

HOLLAND

Oldenburg

Bremen

FORMER BORDER
BETWEEN EAST AND
WEST GERMANY

Elbe

Perleberg

Neuruppin

Wittenberge

Oranienburg

Meppen

Salzwedel

Stendal

Brandenburg

Berlin

Ems

Hannover

Wolfsburg

Osnabrück

Minden

Braunschweig

Magdeburg

Potsdam

Frankfurt

Rheine

Hildesheim

Oder

Münster

Bielefeld

Halberstadt

Dessau

Wittenberg

Lübben

Duisberg

Essen

Dortmund

Göttingen

Nordhausen

Bernburg

Bitterfeld

Cottbus

Hagen

Kassel

Halle

Leipzig

Meissen

Görlitz

Düsseldorf

Mühlhausen

Neisse

Köln

Siegen

Bad Hersfeld

Erfurt

Weimar

Gera

Dresden

Aachen

Marburg

Eisenach

Chemnitz

Bonn

Alsfeld

Suhl

Saalfeld

Zwickau

Koblenz

Giessen

Fulda

Meiningen

Hof

Plauen

Wiesbaden

Frankfurt-am-Main

Coburg

Münchberg

Mainz

Main

Würzburg

Bamberg

Bayreuth

CZECH REPUBLIC

Trier

Bingen

Darmstadt

Bad
Kreuznach

Mannheim

Fürth

Nürnberg

Mosel

Ludwigshafen

Heidelberg

Rothenburg-
o-d-Tauber

Speyer

Heilbronn

Regensburg

Saarbrücken

Karlsruhe

Deggendorf

Baden-Baden

Stuttgart

Straubing

FRANCE

Offenburg

Ulm

Donau

Augsburg

Isar

Passau

Tübingen

Neu-Ulm

Munich

Donau

Biberach

Inn

Freiburg

Tuttlingen

Memmingen

Rhein

Bodensee

Ravensburg

Wangen

Garmisch-
Partenkirchen

Bad Reichenhall

Rheinfelden

Konstanz

Friedrichshafen

Berchtesgaden

SWITZERLAND

AUSTRIA

LICHTENSTEIN

ITALY

POLAND

Oder

on the road with fodor's

A TRIP TAKES YOU OUT OF YOURSELF. Concerns of life at home disappear, driven away by more immediate thoughts—about, say, what marvels will beguile the next day, or where you'll have dinner. That's where Fodor's comes in. We make sure that you know all your options in Munich, so that you don't miss something that's around the next bend just because you didn't know it was there. Mindful that the best memories of your trip might have nothing to do with what you came to see, we guide you to sights large and small. With Fodor's at your side, serendipitous discoveries are never far away.

Our success in showing you every corner of Munich is a credit to our extraordinary writer. **Marton Radkai** is a native New Yorker of Bavarian/Hungarian descent who has lived in Germany and Austria since 1985, working as a travel photographer, translator, editor, and writer for radio and print media. He resides in Munich.

Don't Forget to Write

Your experiences—positive and negative—matter to us. If we have missed or misstated something, we want to hear about it. We follow up on all suggestions. Contact the Pocket Munich editor at editors@fodors.com or c/o Fodor's at 1745 Broadway, New York, New York 10019. And have a fabulous trip!

Karen Cure

Karen Cure
Editorial Director

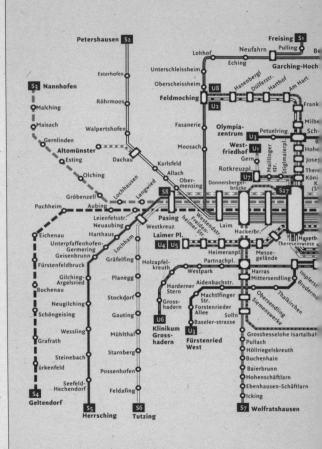

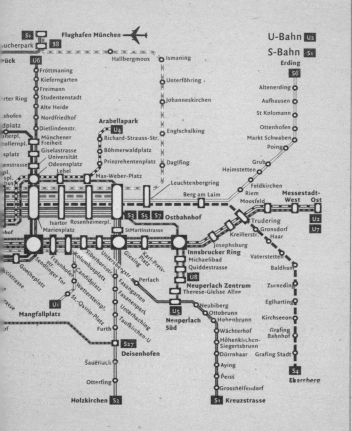

munich

In This Chapter

introducing munich

CHIC AND COSMOPOLITAN, carefree and with a distinct touch of provincial charm. As Bavaria's capital and one of Germany's biggest cities, Munich has more than its share of great museums, architectural treasures, historic sites, and world-class shops, restaurants, and hotels. The same could be said of its abundance of lederhosen and oompah bands. But it's the overall feeling of *Gemütlichkeit*—loosely translated as conviviality—that makes the city so special, with an open-air market here, a park there, and beer halls everywhere.

Munich (*München*) is the single most popular tourist destination for Germans, who mix the city's pleasures with those of the inviting landscapes surrounding it. Munich is kitsch and class, vulgarity and elegance. It exists between two poles, tradition and high-tech, or as the locals say "laptops and lederhosen." It's a city of ravishing baroque and smoky beer cellars, of grand 19th-century architecture and sleek steel-and-glass office buildings, of millionaires and farmers. Germany's favorite city is a place with extraordinary ambience and a vibrant lifestyle all its own, in a splendid setting within view—on a clear day—of the towering Alps.

Munich belongs to the relaxed and sunny south. Call it Germany with a southern exposure—although it may be an exaggeration to claim, as some Bavarians do, that Munich is the only Italian city north of the Alps. Still, there's no mistaking the carefree spirit that infuses the city, and its easygoing approach to life, liberty, and the pursuit of happiness, Bavarian style. The Bavarians refer to this positively un-Teutonic joie de vivre as Gemütlichkeit.

What makes Munich so special? One explanation is the flair for the fanciful that is deeply rooted in Bavarian culture. And no historical figure better personifies this tradition than Ludwig II, one of the last of the Wittelsbachs, the royal dynasty that for almost 750 years ruled over Munich and southern Germany, until the monarchy was forced to abdicate in 1918. While Bismarck was striving from his Berlin power base to create a modern unified Germany, "Mad" Ludwig—also nicknamed the "Dream King"—was almost bankrupting the state's treasury by building a succession of fairy-tale castles and remote summer retreats in the mountains and countryside.

Munich bills itself as *Die Weltstadt mit Herz* (the cosmopolitan city with heart), which it most assuredly is. A survey suggests that most Germans would prefer to live in Munich than where they currently reside, even though it is probably the most expensive place in reunited Germany. This is not to suggest that all Germans subscribe to the "I Love Munich" concept. Certain buttoned-up types—in Hamburg or Düsseldorf, for example—might look down their imperious noses at Munich as just a mite crass and somewhat tacky, and Bavarians as only a few rungs up from the barbarians. So be it.

Munich's stock image is the cavernous beer hall (such as the world-famous Hofbräuhaus) filled with the deafening echo of a brass oompah band and rows of swaying, burly Bavarians in lederhosen being served by frumpy Fraus in flaring dirndl dresses. Every day in different parts of the city, you'll find scenes like this. But there are also many Müncheners who never step inside a beer hall, who never go near Oktoberfest. They belong to the *other* Munich: a city of charm, refinement, and sophistication, represented by two of the world's most important art galleries and a noted opera house; a city of expensive elegance, where high-fashion shops seem in competition to put the highest price tags on their wares; a city of five-star nouvelle cuisine. Munich is the stomping grounds of all kinds of media, from traditional publishing houses to top-notch digital postproduction companies. The concentration of electronics and computer firms—Siemens, IBM, Apple, and the like—in and around the city has turned it into the Silicon Valley of Europe.

Endowed with vast, green tracts of parks, gardens, and forests; grand boulevards set with remarkable edifices; fountains and statuary; and a river spanned by graceful bridges, Munich is easily Germany's most beautiful and interesting city. If the traveler could visit only one city in Germany, this should be it—no question. If you factor in the city's dramatic change over the past decade, a traveler who has not visited for awhile might find a whole new Munich has evolved in the interim. For, quietly and without fanfare, Munich has taken its place as the high-tech capital of Germany, developing into the number-one postindustrial-age center in the country and one of the most important cities in Europe. The concentration of electronics and computer firms— Siemens, IBM, Apple, and the like—in and around the city has turned it into the Silicon Valley of Germany.

PLEASURES AND PASTIMES

BEER AND BEER GARDENS

Munich has more than 100 beer gardens, ranging from huge establishments that seat several hundred guests to small terraces tucked behind neighborhood pubs and taverns. Beer gardens are such an integral part of Munich life that a council proposal to cut down their hours provoked a storm of protest in 1995, culminating in one of the largest mass demonstrations in the city's history. They open whenever the thermometer creeps above 10°C (42°F) or so and when the sun filters through the chestnut trees that are a necessary part of the beer-garden scenery. Most—but not all—allow you to bring along your own food, and if you do, try not to bring something so foreign as pizza or a burger from McDonald's.

A BEER GLOSSARY

The alcohol content of German beers varies considerably. At the weaker end of the scale is the light Munich Helles (3.7% alcohol by volume); stronger brews are Pilsner (around 5%) and Doppelbock (more than 7%).

BOCK: strong beer, which can be light or dark, sweet or dry.

DOPPELBOCK: stronger than Bock, usually dark, and not to be trifled with.

DUNKLES: dark beer, often slightly sweeter or maltier than pale (light) beers.

EXPORT: usually a pale (light-colored) beer of medium strength.

HALBE: half a Mass, the standard beer measure in Bavaria (☞ Mass).

HEFE: yeast.

HELLES: light beer.

KLAR, KRISTALL: wheat beer with the yeast removed.

KLEINES: a small glass of beer (in Bavaria).

LAGER: literally, "store"; that stage of the brewing process when beer matures in the brewery.

LEICHTBIER: beer with low alcohol and calorie content, usually pale in color.

MASS: a 1-liter (almost 2-pint) glass or earthenware mug.

NATURTRÜB: a new term for unfiltered beer, implying the yeast has not been removed.

OBERGÄRIG: top-fermented.

PILS, PILSNER: a golden-color, dry, bitter-flavored beer named after Pilsen, the Czech town where in the 19th century the brewing style was first developed.

POLIZEI STUNDE: literally, "police hour"—closing time; midnight or 1 AM in some big cities, usually earlier in small towns and villages.

PROST: German for "cheers."

RADLER: lemonade and beer mixed.

RAUCHBIER: smoked beer; usually a dark brew with a smoky flavor that comes from infusing the malted barley with beech-wood smoke.

UNTERGÄRIG: bottom-fermented.

WEISSBIER, WEIZENBIER: wheat beer; a highly carbonated, sharp, and sour brew, often with floating yeast particles.

DINING
Old Munich inns (*Gaststätten*) feature solid regional specialties and *gutbürgerliche Küche*, loosely translated as good homey fare. The settings for such victuals include boisterous brewery restaurants, beer halls, beer gardens, rustic cellars, and *Weinstuben* (wine taverns).

The city's snacking tradition is centuries old and a tempting array of food is available almost anytime day or night. The generic term for snacks is *Imbiss*, and thanks to growing internationalism, these come in all shapes, sizes, and national flavors, from the generic *Wiener* (hot dog), to the Turkish *Döner* sandwich (pressed and roasted lamb, beef, or turkey). Following a spate of Chinese places is a small but quality-minded community of sushi bars. Virtually every butcher offers some sort of *Brotzeit* snack, which can range from a modest sandwich to a steaming plate of goulash with potatoes and salad.

Some edibles come with social etiquette attached. Before noon, during what is sometimes called *Frühschoppen* ("early mug"), one eats *Weisswurst*, a tender minced-veal sausage—made fresh daily; steamed; and served with sweet mustard, a crisp roll or a pretzel, and *Weissbier* (wheat beer). As legend has it, this white sausage was invented in 1857 by a butcher who had a hangover and mixed the wrong ingredients. A plaque on a wall in Marienplatz marks where the "mistake" was made. At one time sausage was available only in and around Munich and served only between midnight and noon. Thanks to refrigeration and preservatives, Weisswurst can now be eaten all day in Munich, though some places stop selling them at noon. The better folk use knife and fork to remove the edible part from the skin. The rougher crowd might indulge in *auszuzeln*, using tooth and jaw to suck the innards of the Weisswurst out.

Another favorite Bavarian specialty is *Leberkäs*—literally "liver cheese," although neither liver nor cheese is among its ingredients. It is a spicy meat loaf baked to a crusty turn each morning and served in succulent slabs throughout the day. A *Leberkäs Semmel*—a wedge of the meat loaf between two halves of a crispy bread roll slathered with a slightly sharp mustard—is the favorite Munich on-the-hoof snack. After that comes the repertoire of sausages indigenous to Bavaria, including short thick ones from Regensburg and short thin ones from Nürnberg.

More substantial dishes include *Tellerfleisch*, boiled beef with freshly grated horseradish and boiled potatoes on the side, served on wooden plates (there is a similar dish called *Tafelspitz*). Among roasts, sauerbraten (beef) and *Schweinebraten* (roast pork) are accompanied by dumplings and sauerkraut. *Hax'n* (ham hocks) are roasted until they're crisp on the outside, juicy on the inside. They are served with sauerkraut and potato puree.

Game in season (venison or boar, for instance) and duck are served with potato dumplings and red cabbage. As for fish, the region has not only excellent trout, served either smoked as an hors d'oeuvre or fried or boiled as an entrée, but also the perchlike Rencke from Lake Starnberg.

You'll also find soups, salads, casseroles, hearty stews, and what may well be the greatest variety and the highest quality of baked goods in Europe, including pretzels. And for dessert, put aside the fears of cholesterol and indulge in a bowl of Bavarian cream, apple strudel, or *Dampfnudel*, a fluffy leavened dough dumpling served usually with vanilla sauce. No one need ever go hungry or thirsty in Munich.

MUSIC AND OPERA

Munich and music complement each other marvelously. The city has two world-renowned orchestras (one, the Philharmonic, is directed by the American conductor James Levine), the Bavarian State Opera Company (managed by an ingenious British director, Peter Jonas), wonderful choral ensembles, a rococo jewel of a court theater, and a modern Philharmonic concert hall of superb proportions and acoustics—and that's just for starters.

SHOPPING

Munich has three of Germany's most exclusive shopping streets. At the other end of the scale, it has a variety of flea markets to rival that of any other European city. In between are department stores, where acute German-style competition assures reasonable prices and often produces outstanding bargains. Artisans and artists bring their wares of beauty and originality to the Christmas markets. Collect their business cards—in the summer you're sure to want to order another of those little gold baubles that were on sale in December.

QUICK TOURS

If you're here for just a short period you need to plan carefully so as to make the most of your time in Munich. The following itineraries visit major sights throughout the city. Each is intended to take about four hours—a perfect way to fill a free morning or afternoon.

TOUR 1

Start this central Munich tour on Marienplatz square shortly before 11 AM, when the elaborate Glockenspiel (carillon) in the tower of the neo-Gothic Neues Rathaus (city hall) clanks and whirrs into action. There's a tourist information office in the Rathaus, if you need maps and brochures. The city's original city hall, the Altes Rathaus, is on the eastern edge of the square, but you can only admire it from outside. Exit Marienplatz on the south, along the old cattle market, Rindermarkt, and get a bird's eye view of the city from the top of the tower of St. Peter's Church. At lunchtime, the city's central market, the Viktualienmarkt, is just south of St. Peter's, and you can sample Munich beer and meat specialties at one of the many market stalls. Stroll down Rosental to Sendlingerstrasse, for the one "must-see" Munich church interior: the incredibly ornate 18th-century Asamkirche. Explore the boutique-crammed jumble of streets behind the church, and within five minutes you'll be in the city's shopping-mile, the traffic free Neuhauser-Kaufinger-Strasse mall. Head back east toward Marienplatz, your starting and ending point, but leave time for a visit to the city's cathedral, the Frauenkirche. Its tall brick towers signal the way.

TOUR 2

Marienplatz is again the starting point. Duck through the arches of the former city hall, the Altes Rathaus, turn left into Burgstrasse, and you'll find a peaceful square lined by medieval buildings that were once the site of the original Wittelsbach royal palace, the Alter Hof. Its successor, the Residenz, is a few hundred yards north. Cross Maximilianstrasse and Max-Josef-Platz (the opera house on your right) to reach it. Exploring the Residenz (closed Monday) will take a couple of hours, but afterward stroll north to the royal gardens, the Hofgarten. On the way, take a look at the Feldherrnhalle (an imitation Florentine loggia abused as a Nazi shrine) and the Baroque Theatinerkirche. Finish your tour with coffee at Munich's oldest cafe, the Tambosi, on Odeonsplatz.

TOUR 3

This museum tour starts at the main railway station, the Hauptbahnhof, where there is a tourist information office. Head northwest, through the original botanical gardens, the Alter Botanischer Garten, and continue up Meiserstrasse to Königsplatz. If antiquities are your thing there are two fine museums of Greek, Etruscan and Roman art on either side of the huge square (the Antikensammlungen and the Glyptothek). For something more modern continue up Meiserstrasse, which turns into Arcisstrasse, and on the right you'll find the Alte Pinakothek and Neue Pinakothek, Munich's leading art galleries. Visit Munich's museums in the afternoon, when the school groups have passed through—it will also give you an excuse to end your tour at happy hour in one of the many bars and cafés in this part of Schwabing, the old artists' quarter.

TOUR 4

Lace up walking shoes for this tour through Munich's huge city park, the Englischer Garten. Starting point is Odeonsplatz (U3 and U6 subway stop), which leads into the old royal gardens, the Hofgarten, and thence into the Englischer Garten. On the right as you cross into the park you'll see one of the few remnants of Nazi architecture in Munich—the Haus der Kunst, a major art gallery and home to Munich's top disco, the PI. Return there after dark, if that's your scene, but first introduce yourself to Munich beer at the city's most celebrated beer garden, the Chinesischer Turm (Chinese Tower), named after the replica of a Chinese pagoda that stands incongruously in the midst of leafy English-style parkland. Work up a thirst again with a 1 km walk north to the park's largest stretch of water, the Kleinhesselohesee, where you'll find another more upmarket beer garden. Walk around the lake and head south to Odeonsplatz, trying to synchronize this part of your tour with the sunset behind Munich's steepled city panorama.

In This Chapter

here and there

MUNICH IS A WEALTHY CITY—and it shows. Everything is extremely upscale and up-to-date. At times the aura of affluence may be all but overpowering. But that's what Munich is all about these days and nights: a new city superimposed on the old; conspicuous consumption; a fresh patina of glitter along with the traditional rustic charms. Such are the dynamics and duality of this fascinating town.

THE CITY CENTER

Munich was created in the 12th century as a market town on the "salt road" connecting mighty Salzburg and Augsburg. The Innenstadt, or city center, is younger than some of the surrounding neighborhoods, such as Heuhausen or Haidhausen. The center has been rebuilt so often over the centuries, that it no longer has that homogeneous look that one finds in many other old German towns. Postwar developments often separate clusters of buildings that date back to Munich's origins—and not always to harmonious effect. The outer perimeter of this tour is defined more by your stamina than by ancient city walls.

Numbers in the text correspond to numbers in the margin and on the Munich map.

A Good Walk

Begin your walk through the city center at the **HAUPTBAHNHOF** ①, the main train station and site of the city tourist office, which is next to the station's main entrance. Pick

munich (münchen)

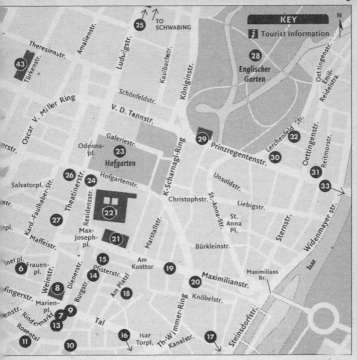

up a detailed city map here. Cross Bahnhofplatz, the square in front of the station (or take the underpass), and walk toward Schützenstrasse, which marks the start of Munich's pedestrian shopping mall, the *Fussgängerzone*, 2 km (1 mi) of traffic-free streets. Running virtually the length of Schützenstrasse is Munich's largest department store, Hertie. At the end of the street you descend via the pedestrian underpass into a vast underground complex of boutiques, shops, and snack bars. Above you is the busy traffic intersection, **KARLSPLATZ** ②, always referred to as Stachus after an inn and beer garden that stood here back in the 19th century. Its fountain area is a favorite place to hang out. Just make sure your wallet is safe.

Ahead stands one of the city's oldest gates, the Karlstor, first mentioned in local records in 1302. Beyond it lies Munich's main shopping thoroughfare, Neuhauserstrasse, and its extension, Kaufingerstrasse. On your left as you enter Neuhauserstrasse is another attractive fountain: a late-19th-century figure of Bacchus. This part of town was almost completely destroyed by bombing during World War II. Great efforts were made to ensure that the designs of the new buildings harmonized with the old city, although some of the modern structures are little more than functional. Though this may not be an architectural showplace, there are redeeming features to the area. Haus Oberpollinger, on Neuhauserstrasse, is one; it's a department store hiding behind an imposing 19th-century facade. Notice the weather vanes of old merchant ships on its high-gabled roof.

Shopping is not the only attraction on these streets. Worldly department stores rub shoulders with two remarkable churches. The first is the **BÜRGERSAAL** ③, which dates to the early 18th century. Farther on comes the **MICHAELSKIRCHE** ④, a Renaissance construction originally built in the 16th century and entirely redone after the war. A part of the pavement near the Michaelskirche is alive with hundreds of tulips in spring. The fountain here features Salome, in honor of the opera of the same name by Munich's famous son Richard Strauss. The massive building next to Michaelskirche was once one of Munich's oldest churches. Originally built in the 13th century for Augustine monks, the edifice was secularized in the early 19th century and today is the **DEUTSCHES JAGD- UND FISCHEREIMUSEUM** (German Hunting and Fishing Museum) ⑤. Opposite is one of Munich's famous brewery inns, the Augustiner Bierhalle. Behind its Renaissance and baroque facade—the establishment occupies two buildings—are vaulted ceilings and a delightful little courtyard decorated with frescoes.

Turn left at the museum onto crescent-shape Augustinerstrasse, and you will soon arrive in Frauenplatz, a quiet square with a shallow, sunken fountain. Towering over it is the **FRAUENKIRCHE** ⑥, Munich's cathedral, whose twin onion domes are the city's main landmark and its symbol. From the cathedral follow any of the alleys heading east, and you'll reach the very heart of Munich, **MARIENPLATZ** ⑦, which is surrounded by stores and dining spots. Marienplatz is dominated by the 19th-century **NEUES RATHAUS** ⑧; the **ALTES RATHAUS** ⑨, a rebuilt medieval building of assured charm, sits more modestly at the eastern entrance of the square. Its pretty tower houses a toy museum.

Hungry? Thirsty? Help is only a few steps away. From the Altes Rathaus, cross the street, passing the Heiliggeistkirche, an early Munich church with a rococo interior added between 1724 and 1730. Heiliggeiststrasse brings you to the jumble known as the **VIKTUALIENMARKT** ⑩, the city's open-air food market, where you can eat a stand-up lunch at any of the many stalls.

From the market follow Rosental and turn left onto Sendlingerstrasse, one of the city's most interesting shopping streets. On the way you'll pass the rear of the **MÜNCHNER STADTMUSEUM** (City Museum) ⑪ at the corner of Oberangerstrasse. As you head down Sendlingerstrasse, on your right is the remarkable **ASAMKIRCHE** ⑫. The exterior fits so snugly into the street's housefronts that you might easily overlook the church were it not for the somewhat incongruous rocks it was built upon. At the end of the street is Sendlinger Tor, a medieval brick gate.

Backtrack up Sendlingerstrasse and turn right onto Rindermarkt (the former cattle market), and you'll be beneath the single, square tower of the **PETERSKIRCHE** ⑬, the city's oldest and best-loved parish church. From the Peterskirche reenter Marienplatz and pass in front of the Altes Rathaus once again to step into Burgstrasse. You'll soon find yourself in the quiet, airy **ALTER HOF** ⑭, the inner courtyard of the original palace of Bavaria's Wittelsbach rulers. A short distance beyond its northern archway, on the north side of Pfisterstrasse, stands the former royal mint, the **MÜNZE** ⑮.

If you'd like to visit some museums, extend your walk by about 10 minutes, returning down Burgstrasse to broad Tal, once an important trading route that entered Munich at the Isartor, a gate restored to its original medieval appearance. A frieze depicts the 1322 battle of Ampfing, during which Munich was saved from an Austrian attack. Cross Isartorplatz into Zweibrückenstrasse, and you'll come to the Isar River. There, on an island, is the massive bulk of the **DEUTSCHES MUSEUM** ⑯, with a gigantic thermometer and barometer on its tower showing the way to the main entrance. Budding scientists and young dreamers will be delighted by its many interactive displays with buttons to push and cranks to turn.

On a sunny day join the locals for ice cream and a stroll along the Isar River, where the more daring sunbathe nude on pebble islands. On a rainy day you can splash around in the Müllersches Volksbad, a restored art nouveau indoor swimming pool at Ludwigsbrücke, opposite the Deutsches Museum. The massive glass-and-brick facade on the hill above the Volksbad belongs to the **GASTEIG KULTURZENTRUM** ⑰, home of the Munich

Philharmonic Orchestra, the main city library, and a variety of theaters, galleries, and cafés.

TIMING

Set aside at least a whole day for this walk, hitting Marienplatz when the glockenspiel plays at 11 AM or noon. Prepare for a big spectator crowd, and try to avoid shopping in the pedestrian zone between noon and 2, when workers on lunch break make for the department stores. The churches along the route each deserve some contemplation inside. Aficionados of hunting or engineering could spend hours in the Deutsches Jagd- und Fischereimuseum and Deutsches Museum.

Sights to See

⑭ ALTER HOF (Old Palace). This palace was the original residence of the Wittelsbachs, the ruling dynasty established in 1180. The palace now serves as local government offices. Something of a medieval flavor survives in the Alter Hof's quiet courtyard in the otherwise busy downtown area. Don't pass through without turning to admire the medieval oriel (bay window) that hides on the south wall, just around the corner as you enter the courtyard. *Burgstr., City Center.*

⑨ ALTES RATHAUS (Old City Hall). This was Munich's first city hall, built in 1474. Its great hall—destroyed in 1944 but now fully restored—was the work of architect Jörg von Halspach. It is used for official receptions and is not normally open to the public. The tower provides a fairytale-like setting for the **Spielzeugmuseum** (toy museum) accessible via a winding staircase. Its toys and dolls are joined by quite a few Barbies visiting from the United States. *Marienpl., City Center, tel. 089/294–001. Museum €3. Daily 10–5:30.*

★ ⑫ ASAMKIRCHE (Asam Church). Munich's most unusual church has a suitably extraordinary entrance, framed by raw rock foundations. The insignificant door, crammed between its craggy shoulders, gives little idea of the opulence and lavish detailing within the small, 18th-century church (there are only 12 rows of pews). Above the doorway St. Nepomuk, a 14th-century Bohemian monk who drowned in the Danube, is being led by angels from a rocky riverbank to heaven. The church's official name is Church of St. Johann Nepomuk, but it is known as the Asamkirche for its architects, the brothers Cosmas Damian and Egid Quirin Asam, who lived next door. Inside you'll discover a prime example of true southern German, late-baroque architecture. Frescoes by Cosmas Damian Asam and rosy marble cover the walls. The sheer wealth of statues and gilding is stunning—there's even a gilt skeleton at the sanctuary's portal. *Sendlingerstr., City Center. Daily 9–5:30.*

③ BÜRGERSAAL (Citizens' Hall). Beneath the modest roof of this unassuming church are two contrasting levels. The Oberkirche (upper level)—the church proper—is a richly decorated baroque oratory. Its elaborate stucco foliage and paintings of Bavarian places of pilgrimage project a distinctly different ambience from that of the Unterkirche (lower level), reached by a double staircase. This gloomy, cryptlike chamber contains the tomb of Rupert Mayer, a Jesuit priest renowned for his energetic and outspoken opposition to the Nazis. *Neuhauserstr. 14, City Center, tel. 089/219–9720. Oberkirche only during services; Unterkirche Mon.–Sat. 6:30 AM–7 PM, Sun. 7–7.*

⑤ DEUTSCHES JAGD- UND FISCHEREIMUSEUM (German Museum of Hunting and Fishing). Fans of the thrill of the chase will be fascinated by this museum. It contains the world's largest collection of fishhooks, some 500 stuffed animals (including a 6½-ft-tall North American grizzly bear), a 12,000-year-old skeleton of an Irish deer, and a valuable collection of hunting weapons. Here you can find the elusive *Wolpertinger*, a legendary Bavarian animal. The brass boar outside the front door is a favorite place for parents to photograph children. *Neuhauserstr. 2, City Center, tel. 089/220–522. €3.50. Daily 9:30–5; until 9 on Mon. and Thurs.*

★ ♻ ⓰ **DEUTSCHES MUSEUM** (German Museum of Science and Technology). Within a monumental building on an island in the Isar River, this museum—filled with aircraft, vehicles, locomotives, and machinery—is an engineering student's dream. The immense collection is spread out over 19 km (12 mi) of corridors, six floors of exhibits, and 30 departments. Not all exhibits have explanations in English, which is why you should skip the otherwise impressive coal-mine labyrinth. The most technically advanced planetarium in Europe has up to six shows daily, and includes a Laser Magic display. An IMAX theater—with a wraparound screen six stories high—shows nature and adventure films. The Internet Café on the third floor is open daily 9–3. To arrange for a two-hour tour in English, call tel. 089/217–9252 two weeks in advance. In mid-2003 a subsidiary Center for Transportation will open on the fairgrounds at the Theresienhöhe (where Oktoberfest is held). By 2005, all the transportation exhibitions will be exhibited in the new halls. *Museumsinsel 1, City Center, tel. 089/21790; 089/2112–5180 to reserve tickets at planetarium and IMAX, www.fdt.de. Museum €5, Planetarium €6.25, IMAX €5.95; combined ticket for planetarium and IMAX €10.25 (admission for some performances is higher). Daily 9 AM–11 PM.*

OFF THE **FRANZISKANERKLOSTERKIRCHE ST. ANNA (FRANCISCAN**
BEATEN **MONASTERY CHURCH OF ST. ANNE)** – This striking example of
PATH the two Asam brothers' work is in the Lehel district. Though less opulent than the Asamkirche, this small Franciscan monastery church, consecrated in 1737, impresses with its sense of movement and its heroic scale. It was largely rebuilt after wartime bomb damage. The ceiling fresco by Cosmas Damian Asam glows in all its original vivid joyfulness. The ornate altar was also designed by the Asam brothers. Towering over the delicate little church, on the opposite side of the street, is the neo-Romanesque bulk of the 19th-century church of St. Anne. You can get to Lehel on Tram 17 or U-bahn 4 or 5 from the city center. *St.-Anna-Str., Lehel, tel. 089/212–1820.*

★ ❻ **FRAUENKIRCHE** (Church of Our Lady). Munich's *Dom* (cathedral) is a distinctive late-Gothic brick structure with two towers that are the city's chief landmark. Each is more than 300 ft high, and both are capped by onion-shape domes. The towers are an indelible feature of the skyline and a Munich trademark by now—some say because they look like overflowing beer mugs.

The main body of the cathedral was completed in 20 years (1474–94)—a record time in those days. The towers were added, almost as an afterthought, in 1524–25. Jörg von Halspach, the Frauenkirche's original architect, is buried here. The building suffered severe damage during Allied bombing and was lovingly restored between 1947 and 1957. Inside, the church combines most of von Halspach's original features with a stark, clean modernity and simplicity of line, emphasized by slender, white octagonal pillars that sweep up through the nave to the tracery ceiling. As you enter the church, look on the stone floor for the dark imprint of a large foot—the *Teufelstritt* (Devil's Footprint). According to lore, the devil challenged von Halspach to build a nave without windows. The architect accepted the challenge. When he completed the job, he led the devil to the one spot in the well-lit church from which the 66-ft-high windows could not be seen. The devil stomped his foot in rage and left the *Teufelstritt*. The cathedral houses an elaborate 15th-century black-marble tomb guarded by four 16th-century armored knights. It is the final resting place of Duke Ludwig IV (1302–1347), who became Holy Roman Emperor Ludwig the Bavarian in 1328. The Frauenkirche's great treasure, however, is the collection of 24 carved wooden busts of the Apostles, Saints, and Prophets above the choir, by the 15th-century Munich sculptor Erasmus Grasser.

The observation platform high up in one of the towers offers a splendid view of the city. But beware—you must climb 86 steps to reach the tower elevator! *Frauenpl., City Center, tel.* 089/290–0820. *Tower* €2. *Tower elevator Apr.–Oct., Mon.–Sat.* 10–6.

⑰ GASTEIG KULTURZENTRUM (Gasteig Culture Center). Sitting high above the Isar River, this striking postmodern, brick cultural complex for music, theater, and film has an open-plan interior and a maze of courtyards and plazas. The center has two theaters, where plays in English are occasionally staged. *Rosenheimerstr. 5, Haidhausen, tel. 089/480–980.*

❶ HAUPTBAHNHOF (Main Train Station). A renovation here has made room for a host of rather fancy sandwich bars. On the underground level you'll find all sorts of shops that remain open even on Sundays and holidays. The city tourist office here has maps and helpful information on events around town. *Bahnhofpl., Leopoldvorstadt, tel. 089/2333–0256 or 089/2333–0257.*

❷ KARLSPLATZ. In 1755, Eustachius Föderl opened an inn and beer garden here, which became known as the Stachus. The beer garden is long gone, but the name has remained. This busy intersection has one of Munich's most popular fountains, a circle of water jets that acts as a magnet on hot summer days when city shoppers and office workers seek a cool place to relax. A semicircle of yellow buildings with tall windows and delicate, cast-iron balconies back the fountain.

★ **❼ MARIENPLATZ.** Bordered by the Neues Rathaus, shops, and cafés, this square is named after the gilded statue of the Virgin Mary that has watched over it for more than three centuries. It was erected in 1638 at the behest of Elector Maximilian I as an act of thanksgiving for the city's survival of the Thirty Years' War, the cataclysmic religious struggle that devastated vast regions of Germany. When the statue was taken down from its marble column for cleaning in 1960, workmen found a small casket in the base containing a splinter of wood said to be from the cross of Christ. *Bounded by Kaufingerstr., Rosenstr., Weinstr., and Dienerstr., City Center.*

❹ MICHAELSKIRCHE (St. Michael's Church). A curious story explains why this sturdy Renaissance church has no tower. Seven years after the start of construction the principal tower collapsed. Its patron, pious Duke Wilhelm V, regarded the disaster as a heavenly sign that the church wasn't big enough, so he ordered a change in the plans—this time without a tower. Completed seven years later, the Michaelskirche was the first Renaissance church of this size in southern Germany. The duke is buried in the crypt, along with 40 other Wittelsbachs, including the eccentric King Ludwig II. A severe neoclassical monument in the north transept contains the tomb of Napoléon's stepson, Eugene de Beauharnais, who married one of the daughters of King Maximilian I and died in Munich in 1824. You'll find the plain white-stucco interior of the church and its slightly barnlike atmosphere soothingly simple after the lavish decoration of the nearby Bürgersaal. *Neuhauserstr. 52, City Center, tel. 089/231–7060. €1. Daily 8–7, except during services.*

⑪ **MÜNCHNER STADTMUSEUM** (City Museum). Wedged in by Oberanger, Rosental, and St.-Jakobsplatz, this museum is as eclectic within as the architecture is without. Though the entire complex was rebuilt in several stages after World War II, the original building dates to 1491 (the front on St.-Jakobsplatz). Inside are instrument collections, international cultural exhibits, a film museum showing rarely screened movies, a photo and fashion museum, a puppet theater, and one of the most pleasant cafés in town. *St.-Jakobspl. 1, City Center, tel. 089/2332–2370, www.stadtmuseum-online.de. €2.50; €4 for special exhibitions. Tues.– Sun. 10–6.*

⑮ **MÜNZE** (Mint). Originally the royal stables, the Münze was created by court architect Wilhelm Egkl between 1563 and 1567 and now serves as an office building. A stern neoclassical facade emblazoned with gold was added in 1809; the interior courtyard has Renaissance-style arches. *Pfisterstr. 4, City Center. Free. Mon.– Thurs. 8–4, Fri. 8–2.*

⑧ **NEUES RATHAUS** (New City Hall). Munich's present city hall was built between 1867 and 1908 in the fussy, turreted, neo-Gothic style so beloved by King Ludwig II. Architectural historians are

When you pack your MCI Calling Card, it's like packing your loved ones along too.

Your MCI Calling Card is the easy way to stay in touch when you travel. Use it to call to and from over 125 countries. Plus, every time you call, you can earn frequent flier miles. So wherever your travels take you, call home with your MCI Calling Card. It's even easy to get one. Just visit **www.mci.com/worldphone** or **www.mci.com/partners**.

EASY TO CALL WORLDWIDE

① Just enter the WorldPhone® access number of the country you're calling from.
② Enter or give the operator your MCI Calling Card number.
③ Enter or give the number you're calling.

		Ireland	1-800-55-1001
Australia ◆	1-800-881-100	Italy ◆	800-17-2401
China	108-12	Japan ◆	00539-121
France ◆	0-800-99-0019	South Africa	0800-99-0011
Germany	0800-888-8000	Spain	900-99-0014
Hong Kong	800-96-1121	United Kingdom	0800-89-0222

◆ Public phones may require deposit of coin or phone card for dial tone. ❱ Regulation does not permit intra-Japan calls.

EARN FREQUENT FLIER MILES

Find America
with a Compass

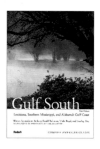

Written by local authors and illustrated throughout
with spectacular color images, the Compass American
Guides reveal the character and culture of more than
40 of America's most fascinating destinations. Perfect
for residents who want to explore their own backyard,
and visitors who want an insider's perspective on
the history, heritage, and all there is to see and do.

Fodor's COMPASS AMERICAN GUIDES

At bookstores everywhere.

divided over its merits, though its dramatic scale and lavish detailing are impressive. Perhaps the most serious criticism is that the Dutch and Flemish style of the building seems out of place amid the baroque and rococo of so much of the rest of the city. The tower's 1904 glockenspiel (a chiming clock with mechanical figures) plays daily at 11 AM, noon, and 9 PM, with an additional performance at 5 PM June–October. As chimes peal out over the square, the clock's doors flip open and brightly colored dancers and jousting knights go through their paces. They act out two events from Munich's past: a tournament held in Marienplatz in 1568 and the *Schäfflertanz* (Dance of the Coopers), which commemorated the end of the plague of 1517. When Munich was in ruins after World War II, an American soldier contributed some paint to restore the battered figures, and he was rewarded with a ride on one of the jousters' horses, high above the cheering crowds. You, too, can travel up there, by elevator, to an observation point near the top of one of the towers. On a clear day the view is spectacular. *Marienpl., City Center. Tower* €1.50. *Mon.–Thurs.* 9–4, *Fri.* 9–1.

⑬ PETERSKIRCHE (St. Peter's Church). Munich's oldest and smallest parish church traces its origins to the 11th century and has been restored in a variety of architectural styles. The rich baroque interior has a magnificent late-Gothic high altar and aisle pillars decorated with exquisite 18th-century figures of the apostles. In clear weather it's well worth the climb up the 300-ft tower—the view includes glimpses of the Alps. The Peterskirche has a Scottish priest who is glad to show English-speaking visitors around. *Rindermarkt, City Center, tel.* 089/260–4828. *Tower* €1.50. *Mon.–Sat.* 9–6, *Sun.* 10–7.

OFF THE **THERESIENWIESE** – The site of Munich's annual beer festival—
BEATEN the notorious Oktoberfest—and of the most hip Christmas
PATH market (the Tollwood) is only a 10-min walk from the Hauptbahnhof or a single stop away by subway (U-4 or U-5). The enormous exhibition ground is named after Princess Therese

von Sachsen-Hildburghausen, who celebrated her marriage to the Bavarian Crown Prince Ludwig—later Ludwig I—here in 1810. The accompanying agricultural fair was such a success that it became an annual event. Beer was served then as now, but what began as a night out for the locals has become a 16-day international bonanza at the end of September and the beginning of October, attracting more than 6 million people each year (it qualifies as an *Oktober* fest by ending the first Sunday in October).

Overlooking the Theresienwiese is a 19th-century hall of fame—one of the last works of Ludwig I—and a monumental bronze statue of the maiden **Bavaria,** more than 100 ft high. The statue is hollow, and 130 steps take you up into the braided head for a view of Munich through Bavaria's eyes. €2.50. *Dec.–Oct., Tues.–Sun. 10–noon and 2–4.*

★ ⑩ **VIKTUALIENMARKT** (Victuals Market). The city's open-air food market has a wide range of produce, German and international foodstuffs, and tables and counters for eating and drinking, which make the area a feast for the eyes as well as the stomach. It's also the realm of the garrulous, sturdy market women who run the stalls with dictatorial authority. Whether here, or at a bakery, *do not* try to select your pickings by hand; ask for help.

OFF THE **VALENTIN-KARLSTADT MUSÄUM** – This museum devoted to
BEATEN the fabulous cabaret artists Karl Valentin (1892–1948) and Liesl
PATH Karlstadt (1892–1960) lies within the tower of the Isartor. It's a must to get a flavor of local culture and color. Valentin, a spookily thin man, was a Munich original, whose absurd humor bashed all conventions. A statue of him and Karlstadt are at Viktualienmarkt. Though much of his wit involves linguistic games, there is much here to catch a sense of genuine, upscale Munich humor, notably a fabulous amount of knickknacks, statues, photographs of Valentin in various off-the-wall poses, and costumes. *Tal 50, City Center/Isarvorstadt, tel. 089/223–266.*

199 Bavarian cents/€1.99. Fri., Sat., Mon., Tues. 11:01–5:29, Sun. 10:01–5:29.

ZAM – Nestled in a passageway just off the Isartor, the ZAM (which stands for Center for Unusual Museums) consists of the private collections belonging to the late Manfred Klauda, a Munich lawyer. There is no specific guiding theme, except perhaps the obsession of a single individual. Exhibitions include collections of chamber pots and bourdaloues (a convenience for women in 17th- and 18th-century clothing), corkscrews, locks, Easter bunnies, pedal cars, perfume bottles, and ephemera relating to Empress Elisabeth of Austria (known as Sissi, the cousin of Ludwig II). Westenriederstr. 41, City Center, tel. 089/290–4121, www.zam-museum.de. €4. Daily 10–6.

ROYAL MUNICH

From the relatively modest palace of the Alter Hof, the Wittelsbachs expanded their quarters northward, where more space was to be found than in the jumble of narrow streets of the old quarter. Three splendid avenues radiated outward from their new palace and garden grounds and fine homes arose along them. One of them—Prinzregentenstrasse—marks the southern end of Munich's huge public park, the Englischer Garten—also the creation of a Wittelsbach ruler. Lehel is an upmarket residential neighborhood that also serves as Munich's museum quarter.

A Good Walk

A good way to start this very long walk is to stoke up with a Bavarian breakfast of Weisswurst, pretzels, and beer at the **HOFBRÄUHAUS** ⑱, perhaps Munich's best-known beer hall, on Am Platzl. Turn right from the Hofbräuhaus for the short walk along Orlandostrasse to **MAXIMILIANSTRASSE** ⑲, Munich's most elegant shopping street. Right opposite you is a handsome city landmark: the Hotel Vier Jahreszeiten, a historic host to traveling princes, millionaires, and the expense-account jet set. Maximilianstrasse was named after King Maximilian II, whose statue you'll see far down on the right. This wide boulevard has many grand buildings, which contain government offices and the city's ethnological museum, the **STAATLICHES MUSEUM FÜR VÖLKERKUNDE** ⑳. The Maximilianeum, on a rise beyond the Isar River, is an impressive mid-19th-century palace where the Bavarian state government now meets.

Turn left on Maximilianstrasse and you'll arrive at Max-Joseph-Platz, a square dominated by the pillared portico of the 19th-century **NATIONALTHEATER** ㉑, home of the Bavarian State Opera Company. The statue in the square's center is of Bavaria's first king, Max Joseph. Along the north side is the lofty and austere south wall of the **RESIDENZ** ㉒, the royal palace of Wittelsbach rulers for more than six centuries.

Directly north of the Residenz, on Hofgartenstrasse, lies the former royal garden, the **HOFGARTEN** ㉓, which was started in the 16th century and eventually achieved its Italian Renaissance look. The plaza in front of the Hogarten is Odeonsplatz. The monument on the southern end is the 19th-century **FELDHERRNHALLE** ㉔, modeled after the familiar Loggia dei Lanzi in Florence. Looking north up Ludwigstrasse, the arrow-straight avenue that begins at the Feldherrnhalle, you'll see the **SIEGESTOR** ㉕, or victory arch, which marks the beginning of Leopoldstrasse. Completing this impressively Italianate panorama is the great yellow bulk of the former royal church of St. Kajetan, the **THEATINERKIRCHE** ㉖, an imposing baroque structure across from the Feldherrnhalle. A few steps down Theatinerstrasse is the **KUNSTHALLE DER HYPO-KULTURSTIFTUNG** ㉗.

Now head north up Ludwigstrasse. Court architect Leo von Klenze designed this first stretch of the generous avenue to give the road to the village of Schwabing a look befitting what had become a kingdom after the Napoleonic wars. In much the same way that Baron Haussmann would later demolish many of the old streets and buildings in Paris, replacing them with stately boulevards, von Klenze swept aside the small dwellings and alleys that stood here and replaced them with severe neoclassical structures such as the Bayerische Staatsbibliothek (Bavarian State Library), the Universität (University), and the peculiarly Byzantine Ludwigskirche. Müncheners either love or hate the architect's high-windowed and formal buildings, which end just before Ludwigstrasse becomes Leopoldstrasse. Another leading architect, Friedrich von Gärtner, took over construction here with more delicate structures that are a pleasant backdrop to the busy street life in summer. Once the hub of the legendary artists' district of Schwabing, Leopoldstrasse still throbs with life from spring to fall, exuding the atmosphere of a Mediterranean boulevard, with cafés, wine terraces, and artists' stalls. In comparison, Ludwigstrasse is inhabited by ghosts of the past.

At the south end of Leopoldstrasse lies the great open quadrangle of the university. A circular area divides into two piazzas named after anti-Nazi resistance leaders: Geschwister-Scholl-Platz and Professor-Huber-Platz. From the University, Leopoldstrasse then continues into Schwabing itself, once Munich's bohemian quarter but now distinctly upscale and chic to the point of being monotonous. Explore the streets of old Schwabing around Wedekindplatz to get the feel of the place. Or enjoy the shops and cafés in the student quarter parallel to Leopoldstrasse. (Those in search of the bohemian mood that once animated Schwabing should head to Haidhausen, on the other side of the Isar River, though it is about to end there, too, owing to gentrification and high rents.)

Bordering the east side of Schwabing is the **ENGLISCHER GARTEN** ㉘. Five kilometers (3 mi) long and 1½ km (about 1 mi) wide, it's Germany's largest city park, stretching from Prinzregentenstrasse, the broad avenue laid out by Prince Regent Luitpold at the end of the 19th century, to the city's northern boundary, where the lush parkland is taken over by the rough embrace of open countryside. Dominating the park's southern border is one of the few examples of Hitler-era architecture still standing in Munich: the colonnaded **HAUS DER KUNST** ㉙, a leading art gallery and home to Munich's most fashionable nightclub, the P 1.

A few hundred yards farther along Prinzregentenstrasse are two other leading museums, the **BAYERISCHES NATIONAL-MUSEUM** ㉚ and the **SCHACK-GALERIE** ㉛, and around the first left-hand corner, on Lerchenfeldstrasse, is a museum of prehistory, the **ARCHÄOLOGISCHE STAATSSAMMLUNG** ㉜, in a modern concrete building appropriately covered with rusting steel Cor-Ten plates.

On a hill at the eastern end of Prinzregentenstrasse, just across the Isar River from the Schack-Galerie, is Munich's well-loved Friedensengel (Angel of Peace), a gilt angel crowning a marble column. Beyond the Friedensengel is another historic home that became a major Munich art gallery—the **MUSEUM VILLA STUCK** ㉝, a jewel of an art-nouveau fantasy wrapped in a sober, neoclassical shell.

TIMING
You'll need a day (and good walking shoes) for this stroll. Set aside at least two hours for a tour of the Residenz. If the weather is good, return to the southern end of the Englischer Garten at dusk, when you'll be treated to an unforgettable silhouette of the Munich skyline, black against the retreating light.

Sights to See

㉜ **ARCHÄOLOGISCHE STAATSSAMMLUNG** (State Archeological Collection). This is Bavaria's principal record of its prehistoric, Roman, and Celtic past. The perfectly preserved body of a ritually sacrificed young girl, recovered from a Bavarian peat moor, is among the more spine-chilling exhibits. Head down to the basement to see the fine Roman mosaic floor. *Lerchenfeldstr. 2, Lehel, tel. 089/211–2402. €4.50; free Sun. Tues.–Sun. 9–4:30.*

③⓪ BAYERISCHES NATIONALMUSEUM (Bavarian National Museum). Although the museum places emphasis on Bavarian cultural history, it has art and artifacts of outstanding international importance and regular exhibitions that attract worldwide attention. The highlight for some will be the medieval and Renaissance wood carvings, with many works by the great Renaissance sculptor Tilman Riemenschneider. Tapestries, arms and armor, a unique collection of Christmas crèches (the *Krippenschau*), and Bavarian and German folk art compete for your attention. *Prinzregentenstr. 3, Lehel, tel. 089/211–2401, www.bayerisches-nationalmuseum.de. €3, €5 for special exhibitions. Tues.–Sun. 9:30–5.*

★ ②⑧ ENGLISCHER GARTEN (English Garden). This virtually endless park, which melds into the open countryside at Munich's northern city limits, was designed for the Bavarian prince Karl Theodor by Benjamin Thompson, later Count Rumford, from Massachusetts, who fled America after having taken the wrong side during the War of Independence. The open, informal nature of the park—reminiscent of the rolling parklands with which English aristocrats of the 18th century liked to surround their country homes—gave the park its name. It has a boating lake, four beer gardens, and a series of curious decorative and monumental constructions, including the Monopteros, a Greek temple designed by von Klenze for King Ludwig I and built on an artificial hill in the southern section of the park. In the center of the park's most popular beer garden is a Chinese pagoda erected in 1789. It was destroyed during the war and then reconstructed. The Chinese Tower beer garden is world famous, but the park has prettier places for nursing a beer: the Aumeister, for example, along the northern perimeter. The Aumeister's restaurant is in an early 19th-century hunting lodge. At the Seehaus, on the shore of the Kleinhesseloher See (lake), choose between a smart restaurant or a cozy *Bierstube* (beer tavern).

The Englischer Garten is a paradise for joggers; cyclists; musicians; soccer players; sunbathers; dog owners; and, in winter, cross-country skiers. The Munich Cricket Club grounds are in the southern section—and spectators are welcome. The park has designated areas for nude sunbathing—the Germans have a positively pagan attitude toward the sun—so don't be surprised to see naked bodies bordering the flower beds and paths. *Main entrances at Prinzregentenstr. and Koniginstr., Schwabing and Lehel.*

㉔ FELDHERRNHALLE (Generals' Hall). This open-sided, pavilionlike building was modeled after the 14th-century Loggia dei Lanzi in Florence and honors three centuries worth of Bavarian generals. Two huge Bavarian lions are flanked by the larger-than-life statues of Count Johann Tserclaes Tilly, who led Catholic forces in the Thirty Years' War, and Prince Karl Philipp Wrede, hero of the 19th-century Napoleonic Wars. The imposing structure was turned into a militaristic shrine in the 1930s and '40s by the Nazis, who also found significance in the coincidence that it marked the site of Hitler's abortive coup, or putsch, which took place in 1923. All who passed it had to give the Nazi salute. Viscardigasse, a tiny alley behind the Feldherrnhalle linking Residenzstrasse and Theatinerstrasse and now lined with exclusive boutiques, was used by those who wanted to dodge the tedious routine. *South end of Odeonspl., City Center.*

㉙ HAUS DER KUNST (House of Art). This colonnaded, classical-style building is one of Munich's few remaining examples of Hitler-era architecture and was officially opened by the führer himself. In the Hitler years it showed only work deemed to reflect the Nazi aesthetic. One of its most successful postwar exhibitions was devoted to works banned by the Nazis. It stages exhibitions of art, photography, and sculpture, as well as theatrical and musical "happenings." The survival-of-the-chicest disco, P 1, is in the building's west wing. *Prinzregentenstr. 1, Lehel, tel. 089/211–270, www.hausderkunst.de. Admission varies. Daily 10–10.*

⑱ HOFBRÄUHAUS. Duke Wilhelm V founded Munich's most famous brewery in 1589. Hofbräu means "royal brew," which aptly describes the golden beer poured in king-size liter mugs. If the cavernous downstairs hall is too noisy for you, try the quiet restaurant upstairs. Americans, Australians, and Italians far outnumber Germans, and the brass band that performs here most days adds modern pop and American folk to the traditional German numbers. *Am Platzl 9, City Center, tel. 089/221–676.*

㉓ HOFGARTEN (Royal Garden). The formal garden was once part of the royal palace grounds. It's bordered on two sides by arcades designed in the 19th century by the royal architect Leo von Klenze. On the east side of the garden stands the new state chancellery, built around the ruins of the 19th-century Army Museum and incorporating the remains of a Renaissance arcade. Its most prominent feature is a large copper dome. Bombed during World War II air raids, the museum stood untouched for almost 40 years as a grim reminder of the war. Nowadays, it is known as Palazzo Prozzi, an untranslatable joke referring to the huge sums that went into rebuilding it, and its ostentatious look.

In front of the chancellery stands one of Europe's most unusual— some say most effective—war memorials. Instead of looking up at a monument, you are led down to a **sunken crypt** covered by a massive granite block. In the crypt lies a German soldier from World War I. The crypt is a stark contrast to the **memorial** that stands unobtrusively in front of the northern wing of the chancellery: a simple cube of black marble bearing facsimiles of handwritten wartime manifestos by anti-Nazi leaders, including members of the White Rose movement. *Hofgartenstr., north of Residenz, City Center.*

㉗ KUNSTHALLE DER HYPO-KULTURSTIFTUNG (Hall of the Hypobank's Cultural Foundation). This exhibition hall for art from antiquity to the most modern studios is in the midst of the commercial pedestrian zone. Chagall, Giacometti, Picasso, and Gauguin are among the artists featured in the past. Its success over the years has led to its expansion, designed by the Swiss architect team Herzog and de Meuron, who also designed London's Tate Modern. *Theatinerstr. 8, City Center, tel. 089/227–817, www.hypo-kunsthalle.de. €14. Daily 10–8.*

LUDWIGSKIRCHE (Ludwig's Church). Planted halfway along the severe, neoclassical Ludwigstrasse is this curious neo-Byzantine/early Renaissance–style church. It was built at the behest of Ludwig I to provide his newly completed suburb with a parish church. It's worth a stop to see the fresco of the *Last Judgment* in the choir. At 60 ft by 37 ft, it is one of the world's largest. *Ludwigstr. 22, Maxvorstadt, tel. 089/288–334. Daily 7–7.*

19 **MAXIMILIANSTRASSE.** Munich's sophisticated shopping street was named after King Maximilian II, who wanted to break away from the Greek-influenced classical style of city architecture favored by his father, Ludwig I. With the cabinet's approval, he created this broad boulevard, its central stretch lined with majestic buildings. It culminates on a rise beyond the Isar River in the stately outlines of the **Maximilianeum**, a lavish 19th-century arcaded palace built for Maximilian II and now the home of the Bavarian state parliament. Only the terrace can be visited.

33 **MUSEUM VILLA STUCK.** This neoclassical villa is the former home of one of Munich's leading turn-of-the-20th-century artists, Franz von Stuck (1863–1928). Renovation of the upstairs rooms, the artist's former quarters, is expected to be completed in 2004. The downstairs is used for special exhibitions. His work, which is at times haunting, at times erotic, and occasionally humorous, covers the walls of the ground floor rooms. *Prinzregentenstr. 60, Haidhausen, tel. 089/4555–5125. Free. Tues.–Sun. 10–6.*

21 **NATIONALTHEATER** (National Theater). Built in the late 19th century as a royal opera house with a pillared portico, this large theater was bombed during the war but is now restored to its original splendor and has some of the world's most advanced stage technology. *Max-Joseph-Pl., City Center, tel. 089/2185–1920.*

★ ㉒ **RESIDENZ** (Royal Palace). Munich's royal palace began as a small castle in the 14th century. The Wittelsbach dukes moved here when the tenements of an expanding Munich encroached upon their Alter Hof. In succeeding centuries the royal residence developed parallel to the importance, requirements, and interests of its occupants. It came to include the Königsbau (on Max-Josef-Platz) and then (clockwise) the Alte Residenz; the Festsaal (Banquet Hall); the Altes Residenztheater/Cuvilliés Theater; the since-destroyed Allerheiligenhofkirche (All Souls' Church); the Residenztheater; and the Nationaltheater.

Building began in 1385 with the **Neuveste** (New Fortress), which comprised the northeast section; most of it burned to the ground in 1750, but one of its finest rooms survived: the 16th-century **Antiquarium,** which was built for Duke Albrecht V's collection of antique statues (today it's used chiefly for state receptions). The throne room of King Ludwig I, the **Neuer Herkulessaal,** is now a concert hall. The accumulated Wittelsbach treasures are on view in several palace museums. The **Schatzkammer** (treasury; €4, a combo ticket with the Residenzmuseum costs €7; Apr.–Oct., Tues., Wed., Fri.–Sun. 9–6, Thurs. 9–8; Nov.–Mar., Tues.–Sun. 9–4) has a rich centerpiece in its small Renaissance statue of St. George, studded with 2,291 diamonds, 209 pearls, and 406 rubies. Paintings, tapestries, furniture, and porcelain are housed in the **Residenzmuseum** (€4; Apr.–Oct., Tues., Wed., Fri.–Sun. 9–6, Thurs. 9–8; Nov.–Mar., Tues.–Sun. 9–4). Antique coins glint in the **Staatliche Münzsammlung** (Residenzstr. 1; €2, free Sun.; Tues.–Sun. 10–5, Thurs. until 6:45). Egyptian works of art make up the **Staatliche Sammlung Ägyptischer Kunst** (Hofgarten entrance; €2.50, free Sun.; Tues. 9–9, Wed.–Fri. 9–4, weekends 10–5).

During the summer, chamber-music concerts take place in the inner courtyard. Also in the center of the complex is the small rococo **Altes Residenztheater/Cuvilliés Theater** (Residenzstr.; €2; Tues.–Sun. 10–4). It was built by François Cuvilliés between 1751 and 1755, and it still holds performances. The French-born

Cuvilliés was a dwarf who was admitted to the Bavarian court as a decorative "bauble." Prince Max Emanuel recognized his latent artistic ability and had him trained as an architect. The prince's eye for talent gave Germany some of its richest rococo treasures. *Max-Joseph-Pl. 3, entry through archway at Residenzstr. 1, City Center, tel. 089/290–671. Closed a few days in early Jan.*

③ SCHACK-GALERIE. Those with a taste for florid and romantic 19th-century German paintings will appreciate the collections of the Schack-Galerie, originally the private collection of one Count Schack. Others may find the gallery dull, filled with plodding and repetitive works by painters who now repose in well-deserved obscurity. *Prinzregentenstr. 9, Lehel, tel. 089/2380–5224. €2.50; free Sun. Wed.–Mon. 10–5.*

㉕ SIEGESTOR (Victory Arch). Marking the beginning of Leopoldstrasse, the Siegestor has Italian origins—it was modeled on the Arch of Constantine in Rome—and was built to honor the achievements of the Bavarian army during the Wars of Liberation (1813–15). The writing on the gable facing the inner city reads: DEDICATED TO VICTORY, DESTROYED BY WAR, ADMONISHING PEACE. *Leopoldstr., Schwabing.*

⑳ STAATLICHES MUSEUM FÜR VÖLKERKUNDE (State Museum of Ethnology). Arts and crafts from around the world are displayed in this extensive museum. There are also regular special exhibits. *Maximilianstr. 42, Lehel, tel. 089/210–1360. €3.50; free Sun. Tues.–Sun. 9:30–5:15.*

㉖ THEATINERKIRCHE (Theatine Church). This mighty baroque church owes its Italian appearance to its founder, Princess Henriette Adelaide, who commissioned it in gratitude for the birth of her son and heir, Max Emanuel, in 1663. A native of Turin, the princess distrusted Bavarian architects and builders and thus summoned a master builder from Bologna, Agostino Barelli, to construct her church. He took as his model the Roman mother church of the newly formed Theatine Order. Barelli worked on the building for 11 years but was dismissed before the project was completed. It was another 100 years before the Theatinerkirche was finished. Its lofty towers frame a restrained facade capped by a massive dome. The superb stucco work on the inside will be covered in scaffolding and dropcloth for part of 2003. The gaping space before the Feldherrnhalle and Theatinerkirche is often used for outdoor stage events. *Theatinerstr. 22, City Center.*

NEED A BREAK? Munich's oldest café, **TAMBOSI** (Odeonspl., Maxvorstadt, tel. 089/224–768), borders the street across from the Theatinerkirche. Watch the hustle and bustle from an outdoor table or retreat through a gate in the Hofgarten's western wall to the café's tree-shaded beer garden. If the weather's cool or rainy, find a corner in the cozy, eclectically furnished interior.

DENKSTÄTTE WEISSE ROSE (Reflecting Place). Siblings Hans and Sophie Scholl, fellow student Alexander Schmorell, and Kurt Huber, Professor of Philosophy, founded the short-lived resistance movement against the Nazis in 1942–43 known as the Weisse Rose (White Rose). All were executed. A small exhibition about their work is in the inner quad of the university, where the Scholls were caught distributing leaflets and denounced by the janitor. *Geschwister-Scholl-Pl. 1, Maxvorstadt, tel. 089/2180–3053. Free. Weekdays 10–4, Thurs. until 9.*

MAXVORSTADT AND SCHWABING

Here is the artistic center of Munich: Schwabing, the old artists' quarter, and the neighboring Maxvorstadt, where most of the city's leading art galleries and museums are congregated. Schwabing is no longer the bohemian area where such diverse residents as Lenin and Kandinsky were once neighbors, but at least the solid cultural foundations of the Maxvorstadt are immutable. Where the two areas meet (in the streets behind the university), life hums with a creative vibrancy.

A Good Walk

Begin with a stroll through the city's old botanical garden, the **ALTER BOTANISCHER GARTEN** ㉞. The grand-looking building opposite the garden's entrance is the Palace of Justice, law courts built in 1897 in suitable awe-inspiring dimensions. On one corner of busy Lenbachplatz, you can't fail to notice one of Munich's most impressive fountains: the monumental late 19th-century Wittelsbacher Brunnen. Beyond the fountain, in Pacellistrasse, is the baroque **DREIFALTIGKEITSKIRCHE** ㉟.

Leave the garden at its Meiserstrasse exit. On the right-hand side you'll pass two solemn neoclassic buildings closely associated with the Third Reich. They first served as the administrative offices of the Nazi Party in Munich. The neighboring building is the Music Academy, where Hitler, Mussolini, Chamberlain, and Daladier signed the prewar pact that carved up Czechoslovakia.

At the junction of Meiserstrasse and Briennerstrasse, look right to see the obelisk dominating the circular **KAROLINENPLATZ** ㊱. To your left will be the expansive **KÖNIGSPLATZ** ㊲, bordered by two museums, the **GLYPTOTHEK** ㊳ and the **ANTIKENSAMMLUNGEN** ㊴, and closed off by the Propyläen, a colonnade framed by two Egyptian pylons.

After walking by the museums, turn right onto Luisenstrasse, and you'll arrive at a Florentine-style villa, the **STÄDTISCHE GALERIE IM LENBACHHAUS** ㊵, which has an outstanding painting collection. Continue down Luisenstrasse, turning right on Theresienstrasse to reach Munich's three leading art galleries, the **ALTE PINAKOTHEK** ㊶; the **NEUE PINAKOTHEK** ㊷, opposite it; and the **PINAKOTHEK DER MODERNE** ㊸. They are as complementary as their buildings are contrasting: the Alte Pinakothek, severe and serious in style; the Neue Pinakothek, almost frivolously Florentine; and the Pinakothek der Moderne, glass-and-concrete new.

After a few hours immersed in culture, end your walk with a leisurely stroll through the neighboring streets of Schwabing, which are lined with boutiques, bars, and restaurants. If it's a fine day, head for the **ELISABETHMARKT,** Schwabing's permanent market.

TIMING
This walk may take an entire day, depending on how long you linger at the major museums en route. Avoid the museum crowds by visiting as early in the day as possible. All of Munich seems to discover an interest in art on Sunday, when admission to most municipal and state-funded museums is free; you might want to take this day off from culture and join the late-breakfast and brunch crowd at the Elisabethmarkt, a beer garden, or at any of the many bars and Gaststätten. Some have Sunday-morning jazz concerts. Many Schwabing bars have happy hours between 6 and 8—a relaxing way to end your day.

Sights to See

★ ❹ **ALTE PINAKOTHEK** (Old Picture Gallery). The towering brick Alte Pinakothek was constructed by von Klenze between 1826 and 1836 to exhibit the collection of old masters begun by Duke Wilhelm IV in the 16th century. It's now judged one of the world's great picture galleries. Among its most famous works are Dürers, Titians, Rembrandts, Rubenses (one of the world's largest collections), and two celebrated Murillos. *Barerstr. 27, Maxvorstadt, tel. 089/2380–5216, www.pinakotheken-muenchen.de. €5; free Sun.; €8 for a combined ticket for the Alte Pinakothek and Neue Pinakothek, valid for 2 days. Tues.–Sun. 10–5, Thurs. until 10.*

❸❹ **ALTER BOTANISCHER GARTEN** (Old Botanical Garden). Munich's first botanical garden began as the site of a huge glass palace, built in 1853 for Germany's first industrial exhibition. In 1931 it shared the fate of a similarly palatial glass exhibition hall, London's Crystal Palace, when its garden burned to the ground; six years later it was redesigned as a public park. Two features from the

1930s remain: a small, square **exhibition hall,** still used for art shows, and the 1933 **Neptune Fountain,** an enormous work in the heavy, monumental style of the prewar years. At the international electricity exhibition of 1882, the world's first high-tension electrical cable was run from the park to a Bavarian village 48 km (30 mi) away. *Entrance at Lenbachpl., Maxvorstadt.*

NEED A BREAK? On the north edge of the Alter Botanischer Garten is one of the city's central beer gardens. It's part of the **PARK-CAFÉ** (Sophienstr. 7, Maxvorstadt, tel. 089/598–313), which at night becomes a fashionable nightclub serving magnums of champagne for €780 a pop. Prices in the beer garden are more realistic.

㊴ ANTIKENSAMMLUNGEN (Antiquities Collection). This museum, which underwent much-needed renovations in 2002, has a collection of small sculptures, Etruscan art, Greek vases, gold, and glass. *Königspl. 1, Maxvorstadt, tel. 089/598–359. €3; combined ticket to Antikensammlungen and Glyptothek €5; free on Sun. Wed., Fri.–Sun. 10–5, Tues. and Thurs. 10–8.*

㉟ DREIFALTIGKEITSKIRCHE (Church of the Holy Trinity). A local woman prophesied doom for the city unless a new church was erected: this striking baroque edifice was then promptly built between 1711 and 1718. It has frescoes by Cosmas Damian Asam depicting all sorts of heroic scenes. *Pacellistr. 10, City Center, tel. 089/290–0820. Daily 7–7, except during services.*

ELISABETHMARKT (Elisabeth Market). Schwabing's permanent market is smaller than the popular Viktualienmarkt, but hardly less colorful. It has a pocket-size beer garden, where a jazz band performs every Saturday from spring to autumn. *Arcistr. and Elisabethstr., Schwabing.*

★ ㊳ GLYPTOTHEK. These Greek and Roman sculptures are among the finest collections in Munich. The small café that expands into the quiet courtyard is a favorite for visitors, which include budding artists practicing their drawing skills. *Königspl. 3, Maxvorstadt, tel. 089/286-100. €3; combined ticket to Glyptothek and Antikensammlungen €5; free Sun. Wed., Fri.–Sun. 10–5, Tues. and Thurs. 10–10.*

36 KAROLINENPLATZ (Caroline Square). At the junction of Barerstrasse and Briennerstrasse, this circular area is dominated by an obelisk unveiled in 1812 as a memorial to Bavarians killed fighting Napoléon. **Amerikahaus** (America House) faces Karolinenplatz. It has an extensive library with many magazines and a year-round program of cultural events. *Karolinenpl. 3, Maxvorstadt, tel. 089/552-5370.*

37 KÖNIGSPLATZ (King's Square). This expansive square is lined on three sides with the monumental Grecian-style buildings by Leo von Klenze that gave Munich the nickname "Athens on the Isar." The two templelike structures are now the Antikensammlungen and the Glyptothek museums. In the 1930s the great parklike square was paved with gray granite slabs, which resounded with the thud of jackboots as the Nazis commandeered the area for their rallies. Although a busy road passes through it, the square has regained something of the green and peaceful appearance intended by Ludwig I.

42 NEUE PINAKOTHEK (New Picture Gallery). This exhibition space opened in 1981 to house the royal collection of modern art left homeless and scattered after its building was destroyed in the war. The exterior of the modern building mimics an older one with Italianate influences. The interior offers a magnificent environment for picture gazing, at least partly due to the natural light flooding in from the skylights. French Impressionists—Monet, Degas, Manet—are all well represented. The 19th-century German and Scandinavian paintings—misty landscapes predominate—are only now coming to be recognized as admirable products of their time. *Barerstr. 29, Maxvorstadt, tel. 089/2380-5195. €5; free Sun. Wed., Fri.–Mon. 10–5, Thurs. 10–10, closed Tues.*

43 PINAKOTHEK DER MODERNE. Munich's ever-delayed new museum will finally open by the end of 2002. The striking glass-and-concrete complex will hold five outstanding art and architectural collections, including modern art, industrial and graphic design, the Bavarian State collection of graphic art, and the Technical University's architectural museum. *Barer Str. 40, Maxvorstadt, tel. 089/2380–5118, www.museum-der-moderne.de. Tues.–Sun. 10–5, Thurs. and Fri. 10–8.*

40 STÄDTISCHE GALERIE IM LENBACHHAUS (Municipal Gallery). Inside this delightful late-19th-century Florentine-style villa, former home and studio of the artist Franz von Lenbach (1836–1904), are renowned works from the Gothic period to the present, including an exciting assemblage of art from the early 20th-century *Blaue Reiter* (Blue Rider) group: Kandinsky, Klee, Jawlensky, Macke, Marc, and Münter. The chambers of Lenbach are on view as well. The adjoining **Kunstbau** (art building), a former subway platform of the Königsplatz station, hosts changing exhibitions of modern art. *Luisenstr. 33, Maxvorstadt, tel. 089/233–0320. €6 (prices vary). Tues.–Thurs., Sun. 10–6, Fri., Sat. 10–8.*

OUTSIDE THE CENTER

☺ **BAVARIA FILMTOUR.** Munich is Germany's leading moviemaking center, and the local Hollywood-style lot, Geiselgasteig, is on the southern outskirts of the city. The Filmexpress transports you on a 1½-hour tour of the sets of *Das Boot* (The Boat), *Die Unendliche Geschichte (The Neverending Story)*, and other productions. Stunt shows are held at 11:30, 1, and 2:30, and action movies are screened in Showscan, the super-wide-screen cinema. Take U-bahn 1 or 2 from the city center to Silberhornstrasse and then change to Tram 25 to Bavariafilmplatz. The Munich transit authority (MVV) offers its own combined ticket for two adults plus three other people under 18 for €22.50; this includes travel. *Bavariafilmpl. 7, Geiselgasteig, tel. 089/6499–2304, www.bavaria-filmtour.de. €10; stunt show €5; showscan €4; combined ticket €17. Nov.–Feb., daily 10–3 (tours only); Mar.–Apr., daily 9–4; May–Oct., daily 9–5.*

BMW MUSEUM ZEITHORIZONTE. Munich is the home of the famous BMW car firm. Its museum, a circular tower that looks as if it served as a set for *Star Wars*, contains not only a dazzling collection of BMWs old and new, but also items and exhibitions relating to the company's social history and its technical developments. It adjoins the **BMW factory** (tel. 089/3895–3308; weekdays, 10–1) on the eastern edge of the Olympiapark. You can see the factory as well, but only with a tour that begins at the museum's box office. Call ahead of time. *Petuelring 130, Milbertshofen, U-bahn 3 to Petuelring, tel. 089/3882–3307. €3. Daily 9–5, last entry at 4.*

BOTANISCHER GARTEN (Botanical Garden). A collection of 14,000 plants, including orchids, cacti, cycads, Alpine flowers, and rhododendrons, makes up one of the most extensive botanical gardens in Europe. The garden lies on the eastern edge of Schloss Nymphenburg park. Take Tram 17 or Bus 41 from the city center. *Menzingerstr. 65, Nymphenburg, tel. 089/ 1786–1350. €2. Oct.–Mar., daily 9–4:30; Apr.–Sept., daily 9–7:30; hothouses daily 9–11:45 and 1–4.*

☾ **HELLABRUNN ZOO.** There are many parklike enclosures, but a minimum of cages at this attractive zoo, which was set up in the early 20th century. Some of the older buildings are in typical art-nouveau style. Care has been taken to group animals according to their natural and geographical habitats. One of the latest additions is the **URWALDHAUS** (rain forest house), which offers guided tours at night (call ahead of time). The 170 acres include restaurants and children's areas. Take Bus 52 from Marienplatz or U-bahn 3 to Thalkirchen, at the southern edge of the city. *Tierparkstr. 30, Harlaching, tel. 089/625–0834, www.zoo-munich.de. €6. Apr.–Sept., daily 8–6; Oct.–Mar., daily 9–5.*

☾ **OLYMPIAPARK** (Olympic Park). On the northern edge of Schwabing, undulating circus-tent-like roofs cover the stadiums built for the 1972 Olympic Games. The roofs are made of translucent tiles that glisten in the midday sun and act as amplifiers for the rock concerts held here. Tours of the park are conducted on a Disneyland-style train throughout the day. An elevator will speed you up the 960-ft **Olympia Tower** (€2.30) for a view of the city and the Alps; there's also a revolving restaurant near the top. Take U-bahn 3 to the park. *tel. 089/3067–2414; 089/3066–8585 for restaurant, www.olympiapark-muenchen.de. Adventure tour €7; stadium tour €4. Main stadium daily 9–4:30; Olympia Tower daily 9 AM–midnight. Tours Apr.–Nov.; grand tour 2 PM, stadium tour 11 AM.*

SCHLOSS BLUTENBURG. An international collection of 500,000 children's books in more than 100 languages fills the shelves in this medieval palace. The library is augmented by collections of original manuscripts, illustrations, and posters. The castle chapel, built in 1488 by Duke Sigismund, has some fine 15th-century stained glass. Take any S-bahn train to Pasing station, then Bus 73 or 76 to the castle gate. The palace is beyond Nymphenburg, on the northwest edge of Munich. *Blutenberg 35, Obermenzing, tel. 089/811–3132. Free. Weekdays 10–5.*

★ **SCHLOSS NYMPHENBURG.** Five generations of Bavarian royalty spent their summers in this glorious baroque and rococo palace. Nymphenburg is the largest palace of its kind in Germany, stretching more than 1 km (½ mi) from one wing to the other. The palace grew in size and scope over a period of more than 200 years, beginning as a summer residence built on land given by Prince Ferdinand Maria to his beloved wife, Henriette Adelaide, on the occasion of the birth of their son and heir, Max Emanuel, in 1663. The princess hired the Italian architect Agostino Barelli to build both the Theatinerkirche and the palace, which was completed in 1675 by his successor, Enrico Zuccalli. Within the original building, now the central axis of the palace complex, is a magnificent hall, the **Steinerner Saal,** extending over two floors and richly decorated with stucco and grandiose frescoes. In the summer, chamber-music concerts are given here. One of the surrounding royal chambers houses the famous **Schönheitsgalerie** (Gallery of Beauties). The walls are hung from floor to ceiling with portraits of women who caught the roving eye of Ludwig I, among them a butcher's daughter and an English duchess. The most famous portrait is of Lola Montez, a sultry beauty and high-class courtesan who, after a time as the mistress of Franz Liszt and later Alexandre Dumas, so enchanted King Ludwig I, that he almost bankrupted the state for her sake and was ultimately forced to abdicate.

The palace is in a park laid out in formal French style, with low hedges and gravel walks extending into woodland. Among the ancient tree stands are three fascinating structures. Don't miss the **Amalienburg** hunting lodge, a rococo gem built by François Cuvilliés, architect of the Altes Residenztheater. The silver-and-blue stucco of the little Amalienburg creates an atmosphere of courtly high life, making clear that the pleasures of the chase here did not always take place outdoors. In the lavishly appointed kennels you'll see that even the dogs lived in luxury. The **Pagodenburg** was built for royal tea parties. Its elegant French exterior disguises a suitably Asian interior in which exotic teas from India and China were served. Swimming parties were held in the **Badenburg,** Europe's first post-Roman heated pool.

Nymphenburg contains so much of interest that a day hardly provides enough time. Don't leave without visiting the former royal stables, now the **Marstallmuseum** (Museum of Royal Carriages; €2.50). It houses a fleet of vehicles, including an elaborately decorated sleigh in which King Ludwig II once glided through the Bavarian twilight, postilion torches lighting the way. On the walls hang portraits of the royal horses. Also exhibited are examples of Nymphenburg porcelain, produced here between 1747 and the 1920s.

A popular museum in the north wing of the palace has nothing to do with the Wittelsbachs but is one of Nymphenburg's major attractions. The **Museum Mensch und Natur** (Museum of Man and Nature; tel. 089/171–382; €1.50, free Sun.; Tues.–Sun. 9–5) concentrates on three areas of interest: the variety of life on Earth, the history of humankind, and our place in the environment.

Smart Sightseeings

Savvy travelers and others who take their sightseeing seriously have skills worth knowing about.

DON'T PLAN YOUR VISIT IN YOUR HOTEL ROOM Don't wait until you pull into town to decide how to spend your days. It's inevitable that there will be much more to see and do than you'll have time for: choose sights in advance.

ORGANIZE YOUR TOURING Note the places that most interest you on a map, and visit places that are near each other during the same morning or afternoon.

START THE DAY WELL EQUIPPED Leave your hotel in the morning with everything you need for the day—maps, medicines, extra film, your guidebook, rain gear, and another layer of clothing in case the weather turns cooler.

TOUR MUSEUMS EARLY If you're there when the doors open you'll have an intimate experience of the collection.

EASY DOES IT See museums in the mornings, when you're fresh, and visit sit-down attractions later on. Take breaks before you need them.

STRIKE UP A CONVERSATION Only curmudgeons don't respond to a smile and a polite request for information. Most people appreciate your interest in their home town. And your conversations may end up being your most vivid memories.

GET LOST When you do, you never know what you'll find—but you can count on it being memorable. Use your guidebook to help you get back on track. Build wandering-around time into every day.

QUIT BEFORE YOU'RE TIRED There's no point in seeing that one extra sight if you're too exhausted to enjoy it.

TAKE YOUR MOTHER'S ADVICE Go to the bathroom when you have the chance. You never know what lies ahead.

Main exhibits include a huge representation of the human brain and a chunk of Alpine crystal weighing half a ton. Take Tram 17 or Bus 41 from the city center to the Schloss Nymphenburg stop. *Notburgastr. at the bridge crossing the Nymphenburg Canal, Nymphenburg, tel. 089/179–080. Schloss Nymphenburg complex (Gesamtkarte, or combined ticket, incl. the Marstall Museum, but not the Museum Mensch und Natur) €7.50; €6.50 in winter, when parts of the complex are closed. Apr.–Sept., daily 9–6; Oct.–Mar., daily 10–4. All except Amalienburg and gardens closed Mon.*

SCHLOSS SCHLEISSHEIM (Schleissheim Palace). In 1597 Duke Wilhelm V decided to look for a peaceful retreat outside Munich and found what he wanted at this palace, then far beyond the city walls but now only a short ride on a train and a bus. A later ruler, Prince Max Emanuel, added a second, smaller palace, the **Lustheim.** Separated from Schleissheim by a formal garden and a decorative canal, the Lustheim houses Germany's largest collection of Meissen porcelain. To reach the palace, take the suburban S-bahn 1 line to Oberschleissheim station and then Bus 292 (which doesn't run on weekends). *Maximilianshof 1, Oberschleissheim, tel. 089/315–5272. Combined ticket for palaces and porcelain collection €2.50. Tues.–Sun. 10–12:30 and 1:30–5.*

SÜDFRIEDHOF (Southern Cemetery). At this museum-piece cemetery you'll find many famous names but few tourists. Four hundred years ago it was a graveyard beyond the city walls for plague victims and paupers. During the 19th century it was refashioned into an upscale last resting place by the city architect Friedrich von Gärtner. Royal architect Leo von Klenze designed some of the headstones, and both he and von Gärtner are among the famous names you'll find there. The last burial here took place more than 40 years ago. The Südfriedhof is a short 10-minute walk south from the U-bahn station at Sendlinger-Tor-Platz. *Thalkirchnerstr., Thalkirchen.*

In This Chapter

eating out

WITH SEVEN MICHELIN-STARRED RESTAURANTS to its credit, Munich claims to be Germany's gourmet capital. It certainly has an inordinate number of fine French restaurants, some with chef-owners who honed their skills under such Gallic masters as Paul Bocuse. For connoisseurs, wining and dining at Tantris or the Königshof could well turn into the equivalent of a religious experience; culinary creations are accorded the status of works of art on a par with a Bach fugue or a Dürer painting, with tabs equal to a king's ransom. Epicureans are convinced that one can dine as well in Munich as in any other city on the Continent.

However, the genuine Munich cuisine is to be experienced in those rustic places that serve down-home Bavarian specialties in ample portions. The city's renowned beer and wine restaurants offer superb atmosphere, low prices, and as much wholesome German food as you'll ever want. They're open at just about any hour of the day or night—you can order your roast pork at 11 AM or 11 PM.

Prices

CATEGORY	COST*
$$$$	over €20
$$$	€15–€20
$$	€10–€15
$	under €10

*per person for a main course at dinner

munich dining

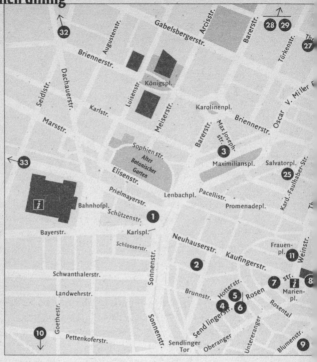

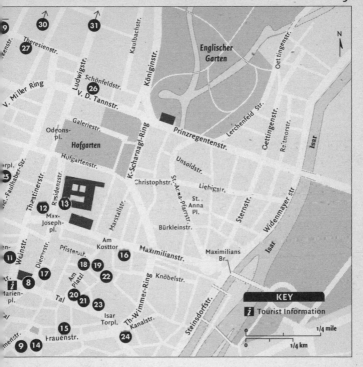

CITY CENTER

$$$$ AM MARSTALL. The exciting menu of this Michelin-starred restaurant combines the best of French and German cuisine—lamb bred on the salt-soaked meadows of coastal Brittany, for instance, or venison from the hunting grounds of Lower Bavaria. Book a window seat so you can while away the time between courses by watching Bavaria's well-heeled shoppers promenading on Maximilianstrasse. *Maximilianstr. 16, City Center, tel. 089/2916–5511. Reservations essential. Jacket and tie. AE, MC, V. Closed Sun., Mon., and holidays.*

$$$$ KÖNIGSHOF. A Michelin star recognizes the reliable old hotel restaurant's place among Munich's finest and most traditional dining rooms. The outstanding menu is French influenced, the surroundings elegant—and if you book a window table you'll have a view of Munich's busiest square, the Stachus, an incandescent experience at night. *Karlspl. 25, City Center, tel. 089/5513–6142. Reservations essential. Jacket and tie. AE, DC, MC, V. No lunch in Aug.*

$$$–$$$$ AUSTERNKELLER. *Austern* (oysters) are the specialty of this cellar restaurant, although many other varieties of seafood—all flown in daily from France—help fill its imaginative menu. The lobster thermidor surpasses that served elsewhere in Munich, while a rich fish soup can be had for less than €5. The fussy, fishnet-hung decor is a shade too maritime, especially for downtown Munich, but the starched white linen and glittering glassware and cutlery lend a note of elegance. *Stollbergstr. 11, City Center, tel. 089/298–787. AE, DC, MC, V. No lunch.*

$$$–$$$$ HALALI. The Halali is an old-style Munich restaurant—polished wood paneling and antlers on the walls—that offers new-style regional specialties, such as venison in juniper-berry sauce and marinated beef on a bean salad. Save room for the homemade vanilla ice cream. *Schönfeldstr. 22, City Center, tel. 089/285–909. Jacket and tie. AE, MC, V. Closed Sun.*

$$$–$$$$ HUNSINGERS PACIFIC. Werner Hunsinger, one of Germany's top restaurateurs, has brought to Munich a reasonably priced restaurant serving eclectic cuisine, borrowing from the Pacific Rim of East Asia, Australia, and North and South America. The restaurant's clam chowder is the best in the city, while another praised specialty is the Chilean-style fillet steak, wrapped in a mantle of onion and eggplant-flavored maize. The many "small dishes" will give you a good panoramic taste of the place. Lunchtime two-course meals cost less than €13. *Maximilianspl. 5, entrance is in Max-Joseph-Str., City Center, tel. 089/5502–9741. AE, DC, MC, V. No lunch weekends.*

$$–$$$$ DUKATZ. ★ A literary and business crowd mixes at this smart bar and restaurant in the Literaturhaus, a converted city mansion where regular book readings are presented. Food includes German nouvelle cuisine, but there is a strong gallic touch here as well as traditional with dishes such as calves' head and lamb tripe. Note the verbal art, some of it by New York artist Jennifer Holzer, such as the statement at the bottom of your cup saying: "More eroticism, gentlemen!" *Salvatorpl. 1, City Center, tel. 089/291–9600. No credit cards.*

$$–$$$$ SPATENHAUS. ★ A view of the opera house and the royal palace complements the Bavarian mood of the wood-paneled and beamed Spatenhaus. The menu is international, however, with more or less everything from artichokes to *zuppa Romana* (alcohol-soaked, fruity Italian cake-pudding). But since you're in Bavaria, try the Bavarian plate, an enormous mixture of local meats and sausages. *Residenzstr. 12, City Center, tel. 089/290–7060. AE, MC, V.*

$$–$$$ GRÜNE GANS. This small, chummy restaurant near the Viktualienmarkt is popular with local entertainers, whose photos clutter the walls. International fare with regional German influences dominates the menu, and there are even a few Chinese dishes. Try the chervil cream soup, followed by calves' kidneys in tarragon sauce. *Am Einlass 5, City Center, tel. 089/266–228. Reservations essential. No credit cards. Closed Sun.*

$$–$$$ HACKERHAUS. The cozy, upscale restaurant belonging to the Hacker brewery (founded in the 15th century) has three floors of wood-paneled rooms. In summer you can order a cheese plate and beer in the cool, flower-bedecked inner courtyard; in winter you can snuggle in a corner of the Ratsstube and warm up on thick homemade potato broth, followed by schnitzel and *Bratkartoffein* (panfried potatoes), or take a table in the Bürgerstube and admire its proud centerpiece, the world's largest beer mug. *Sendlingerstr. 14, City Center, tel. 089/260–5026. AE, DC, MC, V.*

$–$$$ BUXS. This self-service vegetarian place has a full range of salads, excellent entrées, freshly pressed juices and smoothies, and desserts that are worth the caloric splurge. On warm days you can sit outside and watch the Viktualienmarkt activities. *Frauenstr. 9, City Center, tel. 089/291–9195; Amalienstr. 38, Schwabing, tel. 089/280–29940. No credit cards. Closed Sun. No dinner Sat.*

$–$$$ DÜRNBRÄU. A fountain plays outside this picturesque old Bavarian inn. Inside, it's crowded and noisy. Expect to share a table (the 21-ft table in the middle of the place is a favorite); your fellow diners will range from businesspeople to students. The food is resolutely traditional. Try the cream of spinach soup and the boiled beef. *Dürnbräug. 2, City Center, tel. 089/222–195. AE, DC, MC, V.*

$–$$$ ERSTES MÜNCHNER KARTOFFELHAUS. In Munich's First Potato House tubers come in all forms, from the simplest baked potato with sour cream to gratin creations with shrimp and salmon. When potatoes were first introduced to Germany, they were dismissed as fodder fit only for animals or the very lowest strata of society. Frederick the Great was largely responsible for putting them on the dining tables of even the nobility, and now the lowly potato is an indispensable part of the German diet. This restaurant is fun and a great value, too. *Hochbrückenstr. 3, City Center, tel. 089/296–331. Reservations essential. AE, MC, V.*

$–$$$ HAXENBAUER. This is one of Munich's more sophisticated beer restaurants, with a much greater emphasis on the quality of the food than in similar places. Try the *Schweineshaxn* (pork shanks) cooked over a charcoal fire. The two branches consist of the usual series of interlinking rooms with sturdy yet attractive Bavarian decoration. The restaurant at the corner of Sparkassenstrasse and Ledererstrasse has a big traditional noisy beer hall. The Münzstrasse venue is more intimate. *Münzstr. 2 and around the corner at Sparkassenstr. and Ledererstr., City Center, tel. 089/2916–2100 for both sites. AE, MC, V. Münzstr. Haxenbauer is closed Sun.*

$–$$$ HUNDSKUGEL. This is Munich's oldest tavern and also one of the
★ city's smallest. You'll be asked to squeeze together and make room for latecomers looking for a spot at one of the few tables that clutter the handkerchief-size dining room. The tavern dates from 1440 and in many ways doesn't appear to have changed much over the centuries. Even the menu is medievally basic and a bit hit-and-miss, although any combination of pork and potato or sauerkraut can be recommended. *Hotterstr. 18, City Center, tel. 089/264–272. No credit cards.*

$–$$$ MONACO. One of the latest and nicest additions to the Italian scene, the Monaco makes its guests feel at home right away, ensuring returning customers. The decor is simple and unpretentious. Excellent wines on the menu are backed up by a serendipitous selection that the waiter will recommend off the cuff. *Reichenbachstr. 10, City Center, tel. 089/268–141. MC, V.*

$–$$$ SPÖCKMEIER. This rambling, solidly Bavarian beer restaurant spread over three floors, including a snug *Keller* (cellar), is famous for its homemade Weisswurst. If you've just stopped in for a snack and don't fancy the fat breakfast sausage, order coffee and pretzels or, in the afternoon, a wedge of cheesecake. The daily changing menu also offers more than two dozen hearty main-course dishes and a choice of four draft beers. The house *Eintopf* (a rich broth of noodles and pork) is a meal in itself. The Spöckmeier is only 50 yards from Marienplatz; on sunny summer days tables are set outside in the car-free street. *Rosenstr. 9, City Center, tel. 089/268–088. AE, DC, MC, V.*

$–$$$ WEINHAUS NEUNER. Munich's oldest wine tavern serves good
food as well as superior wines in its three nooks: the wood-panel
restaurant, the Weinstübl, and the small bistro. The choice of food
is remarkable, from nouvelle German to old-fashioned country.
Specialties include home-smoked beef and salmon. *Herzogspitalstr.
8, City Center, tel. 089/260–3954. AE, MC, V. Closed Sun.*

$$ WEINSTADL. At the end of a small alley off a busy shopping street
and overlooked by most passersby, the historic 16th-century
Weinstadl is well worth hunting out. In summer the courtyard beer
garden is a cool delight. A brass-studded oaken door opens onto
a vaulted dining room where traditional Bavarian fare is served
at bench-lined tables. A lunchtime menu and a glass of excellent
beer costs around €10. The cellar, reached via a winding staircase,
features live music on Friday and Saturday evenings. *Burgstr. 5, City
Center, tel. 089/2280–7420. AE, DC, MC.*

$–$$ RATSKELLER. Munich's Ratskeller under the city hall is known for
its goulash soup. Seat yourself—the space is cavernous, and the
setting includes vaulted stone ceilings, alcoves, banquettes, and
wrought-iron work. An atmospheric tavern serves fine Franconian
wine from Würzburg's famous Juliusspital at a price that can't be
matched in Munich. *Marienpl. 8, City Center, tel. 089/219–9890. AE,
MC, V.*

$–$$ HOFBRÄUHAUS. The pounding oompah band draws the curious
into this father of all beer halls, where singing and shouting
drinkers contribute to the earsplitting din. This is no place for the
fainthearted, although a trip to Munich would be incomplete
without a look. Upstairs is a quieter restaurant. In March, May,
and September ask for one of the special, extra-strong seasonal
beers (Starkbier, Maibock, Märzen), which complement the heavy,
traditional Bavarian fare. *Am Platzl 9, City Center, tel. 089/221–676
or 089/290–1360. Reservations not accepted. V.*

$–$$ NÜRNBERGER BRATWURST GLÖCKL AM DOM. Munich's most
original beer tavern is dedicated to a specialty from a rival city,

Nuremberg, whose delicious *Nürnberger Bratwürste* (finger-size sausages) form the staple dish of the menu. They're served by a busy team of friendly waitresses dressed in Bavarian dirndls, who flit between the crowded tables with remarkable agility. In summer tables are placed outside under a bright awning and in the shade of the nearby Frauenkirche. In winter the mellow dark-paneled dining rooms provide relief from the cold. *Frauenpl. 9, City Center, tel. 089/220–385. DC, MC, V.*

$–$$ PFÄLZER WEINPROBIERSTUBE. A warren of stone-vaulted rooms, wooden tables, flickering candles, dirndl-clad waitresses, and a vast range of wines add up to an experience as close to everyone's image of timeless Germany as you're likely to get. The wines are mostly from the *Pfalz* (Palatinate), as are many of the specialties on the limited menu. Here you'll find former chancellor Kohl's favorite dish, *Saumagen* (meat loaf, spiced with herbs and cooked in a pig's stomach). This place is an excellent value, considering the central location. *Residenzstr. 1, City Center, tel. 089/225–628. Reservations not accepted. No credit cards.*

$–$$ PRINZ MYSHKIN. This sophisticated vegetarian restaurant spices
★ up predictable cuisine by mixing Italian and Asian influences. You have the choice of antipasti, homemade gnocchi, tofu and stir-fried dishes, and excellent wines. If your hunger is only moderate, you can get half portions. The airy room has a majestically vaulted ceiling, and there's always some art exhibited to feed the eye and mind. *Hackenstr. 2, City Center, tel. 089/265–596. MC, V.*

$–$$ WEISSES BRÄUHAUS. If you have developed a taste for Munich's Weissbier, this is the place to enjoy it. The flavorful Weisse (from the Schneider brewery) is served with hearty Bavarian dishes, mostly variations of pork and dumplings or cabbage, by some of Munich's friendlier waitresses, good-humored women in crisp black dresses, who appear to match the art nouveau features of the restaurant's beautifully restored interior. *Tal 7, City Center, tel. 089/299–875. No credit cards.*

MAXVORSTADT

$ COHEN'S. Reviving the old Jewish Central-European tradition of good, healthy cooking together with hospitality and good cheer seems to be the underlying principle at Cohen's. Dig into a few hearty latkes, a steaming plate of Chulend stew, or a standard gefilte fish doused with excellent Golan wine from Israel. The kitchen is open from 12:30 PM to about 10:30 PM, and if the atmosphere is good, patrons might just be able to hang out chattering until the wee hours. Klezmer singers perform on Friday evenings. *Theresienstr. 31, Maxvorstadt, tel. 089/280–9545. AE, MC, V.*

LEHEL

$–$$ GASTHAUS ISARTHOR. The old-fashioned "Wirtshaus," where the innkeeper has his patrons in his sights and keeps the mood going, lives on in this old, wedge-shape dining room. For Rainer Menne, who hails from Salzburg, Austria, having a social mix at his simple wooden tables is the secret of a good establishment— actors, government officials, apprentice craftspersons, journalists, and retirees sit side by side. Besides pork roasts, roast beef with onions, boiled beef, and the like, the house specialty is the Augustiner beer from a wooden barrel, tapped once a day at around 6 PM. When the barrel is empty, that's it for the day. *Kanalstr. 2, Lehel, tel. 089/227–753. No credit cards.*

SCHWABING

$$$$ TANTRIS. Chef Hans Haas has kept this restaurant with a modernist
★ look among the top five dining establishments in Munich. He's been named the country's best chef by Germany's premier food critics in the past. You, too, will be impressed by the exotic nouvelle cuisine on the menu, including such specialties as shellfish and creamed potato soup and roasted wood pigeon with scented rice. But you may wish to ignore the bare concrete surroundings and the garish orange-and-yellow decor. *Johann-Fichte-Str. 7, Schwabing, tel. 089/361–9590. Reservations essential. Jacket and tie. AE, DC, MC, V. Closed Sun.*

$$–$$$ BISTRO CEZANNE. You're in for French-Provençal dining at this truly Gallic bistro-restaurant in the heart of Munich's former bohemian quarter, Schwabing. Owner-chef Patrick Geay learned his craft from some of Europe's best teachers. His regularly changing blackboard menu features the freshest market products, with vegetables prepared as only the French can. Among the fish dishes, the scallops melt in the mouth, while the coq au vin will conquer the greatest hungers. Reservations are advised. *Konradstr. 1, Schwabing, tel. 089/391–805. AE, DC, MC, V.*

$–$$ BAMBERGER HAUS. The faded elegance of this historic house on the edge of Schwabing's Luitpold Park disguises an up-to-date kitchen, which conjures up inexpensive dishes of modern flair and imagination. Vegetarians are well catered to with cheap and filling gratins. The cellar beer tavern serves one of the best ales in town. In summer reserve a table on the terrace and eat under chestnut trees with a view of the park. *Brunnerstr. 2, Schwabing, tel. 089/308–8966. AE, DC, MC, V.*

$–$$ MAX-EMANUEL-BRAUEREI. This historic old brewery tavern is a great value, with Bavarian dishes rarely costing more than €10; at lunchtime that amount will easily cover the cost of an all-you-can-eat buffet including a couple of beers. The main dining room has a stage, so the bill often covers a cabaret or jazz concert. In summer take a table outside in the secluded little beer garden tucked amidst the apartment blocks. *Adalbertstr. 33, Schwabing, tel. 089/271–5158. AE, MC.*

LEOPOLDVORSTADT

$–$$$ AUGUSTINER KELLER. This 19th-century establishment is the flagship beer restaurant of one of Munich's oldest breweries. The decor emphasizes wood—from the refurbished parquet floors to the wood barrels from which the beer is drawn. The menu changes daily and offers a full range of Bavarian specialties, but try to order Tellerfleisch, served on a big wooden board. Follow that with a couple of *Dampfnudeln* (yeast dumpling served

Eating Well Is the Best Revenge

Eating out is a major part of every travel experience. It's a chance to explore flavors you don't find at home. And often the walking you do on vacation means that you can dig in without guilt.

START AT THE TOP By all means take in a really good restaurant or two while you're on the road. A trip is a time to kick back and savor the pleasures of the palate. Read up on the culinary scene before you leave home. Check out representative menus on the Web—some chefs have gone electronic. And ask friends who have just come back. Then reserve a table as far in advance as you can, remembering that the best establishments book up months in advance. Remember that some good restaurants require you to reconfirm the day before or the day of your meal. Then again, some really good places will call you, so make sure to leave a number where you can be reached.

ADVENTURES IN EATING A trip is the perfect opportunity to try food you can't get at home. So leave yourself open to try an ethnic food that's not represented where you live or to eat fruits and vegetables you've never heard of. One of them may become your next favorite food.

BEYOND GUIDEBOOKS You can rely on the restaurants you find in these pages. But also look for restaurants on your own. When you're ready for lunch, ask people you meet where they eat. Look for tiny holes-in-the-wall with a loyal following and the best burgers or crispiest pizza crust. Find out about local chains whose fame rests upon a single memorable dish. There's hardly a food-lover who doesn't relish the chance to share a favorite place. It's fun to come up with your own special find—and asking about food is a great way to start a conversation.

SAMPLE LOCAL FLAVORS Do check out the specialties. Is there a special brand of ice cream or a special dish that you simply must try?

HAVE A PICNIC Every so often eat al fresco. Grocery shopping gives you a whole different view of a place.

with custard), and you won't feel hungry again for 24 hours. *Arnulfstr. 52, Leopoldvorstadt, tel. 089/594–393. AE, MC, V.*

$–$$ CAFÉ AM BEETHOVENPLATZ. Classical music accompanies excellent fare on Mondays and Tuesdays. An international breakfast menu is served daily (on Sunday with live classic music as well), followed by suitably creative lunch and dinner menus. The pork is supplied by a farm where the free-range pigs are fed only the best natural fodder—so the *Schweinsbraten* (roast pig) is recommended. Reservations are advised as a young and intellectual crowd fills the tables quickly. *Goethestr. 51 (am Beethovenpl.), Leopoldvorstadt, tel. 089/5440–4348. AE, MC, V.*

NEUHAUSEN

$–$$ LEONROD. Turkish food is second nature to Munich. This little establishment at the corner of Albrechtstrasse and Leonrodstrasse in the Neuhausen district (U1 to Rotkreuzplatz and then the 33 bus or 12 tram to Albrechtstrasse) attracts many a local for Turkish pizza or a lamb stew, or simply a delicious plate of warm starters. Portions are generous. Adding to the simple decor (a mural depicting a Turkish countryside) is a belly dancer, who heats up the room on Wednesday and Saturday nights. *Leonrodstr. 45, Neuhausen, tel. 089/123–5661. AE, DC, MC, V.*

In This Chapter

shopping

MUNICH HAS AN IMMENSE CENTRAL SHOPPING AREA, a 2-km (1-mi) *Fussgängerzone* (pedestrian zone) stretching from the train station to Marienplatz and north to Odeonsplatz. The two main streets here are Neuhauserstrasse and Kaufingerstrasse, the sites of most major department stores. For upscale shopping, Maximilianstrasse, Residenzstrasse, and Theatinerstrasse are unbeatable and contain a fine array of classy and tempting stores that are the equal of any in Europe. Schwabing, north of the university, has several of the city's most intriguing and offbeat shopping streets—Schellingstrasse and Hohenzollernstrasse are two to try. Elisabethplatz holds Schwabing's daily produce market.

Just south of Marienplatz, the Viktualienmarkt is the place to shop for groceries from cheese to sausages, to flowers and wine. A visit here is more than just collecting picnic makings; it's central to an understanding of the Müncheners' easy-come-easy-go nature.

ANTIQUES

Bavarian antiques—from a chipped pottery beer mug to a massive farmhouse dresser—are found in the many small shops around the Viktualienmarkt, including on Westenriederstrasse, just south of the market. At Number 8 Westenriederstrasse, a building houses three antiques shops packed from floor to ceiling with curios, including a great collection of ancient dolls and toys. Also try the area north of the university—Türkenstrasse, Theresienstrasse, and Barerstrasse are all filled with antiques stores.

munich shopping

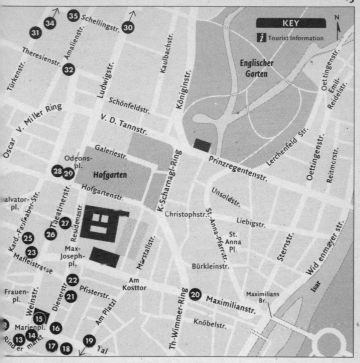

KEY

i Tourist Information

N

Englischer Garten

Schellingstr.

Theresienstr.

Amalienstr.

Türkenstr.

Ludwigstr.

Oscar V. Miller Ring

Schönfeldstr.

V. D. Tannstr.

Kaulbachstr.

Königinstr.

Oettingenstr.

Reidelstr.

Emil-

Lerchenfeld Str.

Oettingenstr.

Reitmorstr.

Galeriestr.

Odeons-pl.

Hofgarten

Hofgartenstr.

Hofgartenstr.

K-Scharnagl-Ring

Prinzregenstr.

alvator-pl.

Kard.-Fa.haber-Str.

Theatinerstr.

Residenzstr.

Maffeistrasse

Max-Joseph-pl.

Marstallstr.

Christophstr.

St.-Anna-Pl.

St. Anna-Pfarrstr.

Unsoldstr.

Liebigstr.

Sternstr.

Wid enmayer str.

Isar

Frauen-pl.

Weinstr.

Dienerstr.

Pfisterstr.

Am Kosttor

Th-Wimmer-Ring

Bürkleinstr.

Maximilianstr.

Maximilians Br.

Marienpl.

Rind er markt

Am Platzl

Tal

Knöbelstr.

Strictly for window-shopping—unless you're looking for something really rare and special, and money's no object—are the exclusive shops lining Prannerstrasse, at the rear of the Hotel Bayerischer Hof. Interesting and inexpensive antiques and assorted junk from all over eastern Europe are laid out at the weekend flea markets beneath the Donnersberger railway bridge on Arnulfstrasse (along the northern side of the Hauptbahnhof).

In **ANTIKE UHREN EDER** (Hotel Bayerischer Hof, Prannerstr. 4, City Center, tel. 089/220–305), the silence is broken only by the ticking of dozens of highly valuable German antique clocks and by discreet negotiation over the high prices. The **ANTIKE UHREN H. SCHLEY** (Kardinal-Faulhaber-Str. 14a, City Center, tel. 089/226–188) specializes in antique clocks. Nautical items or ancient sports equipment (golf clubs, for instance) fill the **CAPTAIN'S SALOON** (Westenriederstr. 31, City Center, tel. 089/221–015). German antique silver and porcelain are the specialty of **ROMAN ODESSER** (Westenriederstr. 16, City Center, tel. 089/226–388). For Munich's largest selection of dolls and marionettes, head to **DIE PUPPENSTUBE** (Luisenstr. 68, Maxvorstadt, tel. 089/272–3267).

DEPARTMENT STORES AND MALLS

HERTIE (Bahnhofpl. 7, Leopoldvorstadt, tel. 089/55120), commanding an entire city block between the train station and Karlsplatz, is the largest and, some claim, the best department store in the city. The basement has a high-class delicatessen with champagne bar and a stand-up bistro offering a daily changing menu that puts many high-price Munich restaurants to shame. Hertie's **Schwabing branch** (Münchner-Freiheit, Schwabing, tel. 089/381–060) is a high-gloss steel-and-glass building. **KARSTADT** (Neuhauserstr. 18, City Center, tel. 089/290–230), in the 100-year-old Haus Oberpollinger, at the start of the Kaufingerstrasse shopping mall, is another upscale department store, with a very wide range of Bavarian arts and crafts. Karstadt also has a Schwabing branch, **Karstadt am Nordbad** (Schleissheimerstr. 93, Schwabing, tel. 089/13020). **KAUFHOF**'s two central Munich stores (Karlspl. 21–24, City Center, tel. 089/51250; Corner Kaufingerstr. and Marienpl., City Center, tel. 089/231–851) offer a variety of goods in the middle price range. The end-of-season sales are bargains.

LUDWIG BECK (Marienpl. 11, City Center, tel. 089/236–910) is considered a step above other department stores by Müncheners. It's packed from top to bottom with highly original wares—from fine feather boas to roughly finished Bavarian pottery. In December a series of booths, each delicately and lovingly decorated, is occupied by craftspeople turning out traditional German toys and decorations. **HIRMER** (Kaufingerstr. 28, City Center, tel. 089/236–830) has Munich's most comprehensive collection of German-made men's clothes, with a markedly friendly and knowledgeable staff. **K & I RUPPERT** (Kaufingerstr. 15, City Center, tel. 089/231–1470) has a fashionable range of German-made clothes in the lower price brackets.

The main pedestrian area has two malls. The aptly named **ARCADE** (Neuhauserstr. 5, City Center) is where the young find the best designer jeans and chunky jewelry. **KAUFINGER TOR** (Kaufingerstr. 117, City Center) has several floors of boutiques and cafés packed neatly together under a high glass roof.

FOLK COSTUMES

If you want to deck yourself out in lederhosen or a dirndl or affect a green loden coat and little pointed hat with feathers, you have a wide choice in the Bavarian capital. Much of the fine loden clothing on sale at **LODENFREY** (Maffeistr. 7–9, City Center, tel. 089/210–390) is made at the company's own factory, on the edge of the Englischer Garten. **WALLACH** (Residenzstr. 3, City Center, tel. 089/220–871) has souvenirs downstairs and shoes and clothing upstairs (though no children's wear). The tiny **LEDERHOSEN WAGNER** (Tal 2, City Center, tel. 089/225–697), right up against the Heiliggeist Church, carries lederhosen, woolen sweaters called *Walk* (not loden), and children's clothing.

GIFT IDEAS

Munich is a city of beer, and items related to its consumption are obvious choices for souvenirs and gifts. Munich is also the home of the famous Nymphenburg Porcelain factory. **DALLMAYR** (Dienerstr. 014–15, City Center, tel. 089/21350) is an elegant gourmet food store, with delights ranging from the most exotic fruits to English jams, served by efficient Munich matrons in smart blue-and-white-linen costumes. The store's famous specialty is coffee, with more than 50 varieties to blend as you wish. There's also an enormous range of breads and a temperature-controlled cigar room. Visit **LUDWIG MORY** (Marienpl. 8, City Center, tel. 089/224–542) for items relating to beer, from mugs of all shapes and sizes and in all sorts of materials, to warmers for those who don't like their beer too cold. Antique mugs and other beer paraphernalia can be found at **ULRICH SCHNEIDER'S** little shop (Radlsteg 2, off Tal, City Center). Check into **SEBASTIAN WESELY** (Rindermarkt 1 [am Peterspl.], City Center, tel. 089/264–519) for beer-related vessels and schnapps glasses (*Stampferl*), walking sticks, scarves, and napkins with the famous Bavarian blue-and-white lozenges. If you've been to the Black Forest and forgot to equip yourself with a clock, or if you need a good Bavarian souvenir, try **MAX KRUG** (Neuhauserstr. 2, City Center, tel. 089/224–501) in the pedestrian zone. Another specialist for some contemporary Bavarica—pipes, nutcrackers, watch chains, beer mugs—is in the same building as Max Krug: **HERRMANN GESCHENKE** (Neuhauserstr. 2, City Center, tel. 089/229–308).

The **NYMPHENBURG STORE** (corner of Odeonspl. and Briennerstr., Maxvorstadt, tel. 089/282–428) resembles a drawing room of the Munich palace, with dove-gray soft furnishings and the delicate, expensive porcelain safely locked away in bowfront cabinets. You can buy direct from the factory on the grounds of **Schloss Nymphenburg** (Nördliches

Schlossrondell 8, Nymphenburg, tel. 089/1791–9710). For Dresden and Meissen ware, go to **KUNSTRING MEISSEN** (Briennerstr. 4, Maxvorstadt, tel. 089/281–532).

Bavarian craftspeople have a showplace of their own, the **BAYERISCHER KUNSTGEWERBE-VEREIN** (Pacellistr. 6–8, City Center, tel. 089/290–1470); here you'll find every kind of handicraft, from glass and pottery to textiles. **KUNST UND SPIEL** (Leopoldstr. 49, Schwabing, tel. 089/381–6270) has a fine selection of toys and clothing for children, and various other handcrafted items. **LEHMKUHL** (Leopoldstr. 45, Schwabing, tel. 089/3801–5013), one of Munich's finest bookshops, also sells beautiful cards. In an arcade of the Neues Rathaus is tiny **JOHANNA DAIMER FILZE ALLER ART** (Dienerstr., City Center, tel. 089/776–984), a shop selling every kind and color of felt imaginable. For an unusual gift of genuine art made of "alternative materials," try **GALERIE BIRO** (Zieblandstr. 19, Schwabing, tel. 089/273–0686). The works are by no means inexpensive, but they are crafted by the top artists working with unusual materials, from Bakelite to plywood. The gallery is closed Sunday through Tuesday.

OTTO KELLNBERGER'S HOLZHANDLUNG (Heiliggeiststr. 7–8, City Center, tel. 089/226–479) specializes in wooden crafts. Looking for that pig's-bristle brush to get to the bottom of tall champagne glasses? **GESCHENK ALM** (Heiliggeiststr. 7–8, City Center, tel. 089/226–479) has nooks and crannies filled with brushes of every kind.

OBLETTER'S (Karlspl. 11–12, City Center, tel. 089/5508–9510) has two extensive floors of toys, many of them handmade playthings of great charm and quality. From November's end until December 24, the open-air stalls of the **CHRISTKINDLMARKT** (Marienpl., City Center) are a great place to find gifts and warm up with mulled wine. Two other perennial Christmas market favorites are those in Schwabing (Münchner-Freiheit Square) and at the Chinese Tower, in the middle of the Englischer Garten.

In This Chapter

outdoor activities and sports

IN THE HUGE, ROLLING ENGLISCHER GARTEN you can cross-country ski or sunbathe nude, depending on the season. The **OLYMPIAPARK** (U-bahn: Olympiazentrum), built for the 1972 Olympics, is one of the largest sports and recreation centers in Europe. For general information about sports opportunities in and around Munich contact the sports emporium **SPORT SCHECK** (Sendlingerstr. 6, City Center, tel. 089/21660). The big store not only sells every kind of equipment but is very handy with advice.

BEACHES AND WATER SPORTS

There is sailing and windsurfing on both the Ammersee and the Starnbergersee (☞ Side Trips). Windsurfers should pay attention to restricted areas at bathing beaches. Information on sailing is available from **BAYERISCHER SEGLER-VERBAND** (Georg-Brauchle-Ring 93, Moosach, tel. 089/1570–2366). For information on windsurfing, contact **VERBAND DER DEUTSCHEN WINDSURFING SCHULEN** (Weilheim, tel. 0881/5267).

GOLF

The **MUNICH GOLF CLUB** has several courses that admit visitors on weekdays. Visitors must be members of a club at home. It has one 18-hole course (tel. 08123/93080) in Eschenried north of the city. The greens fee is €50 (€80 on weekends and holidays). The **GOLFZENTRUM MÜNCHEN-RIEM** (tel. 089/9450–0800) to the east of Munich on the way to the congressional center at Riem. The greens fee is €35, €40 on weekends and holidays.

ICE-SKATING

Depending on weather conditions, there's outdoor skating in winter on the lake in the Englischer Garten and on the Nymphenburger Canal, where you can also go curling (*Eisstockschiessen*) by renting equipment from little wooden huts, which also sell hot drinks. Players rent sections of machine-smoothed ice on the canal. Watch out for signs reading GEFAHR (danger), warning you of thin ice. Additional information is available from **BAYERISCHER EISSPORTVERBAND** (Georg-Brauchle-Ring 93, Moosach, tel. 089/157–9920). The **EISSPORTSTADION** in Olympiapark (Spiridon-Louis-Ring 3, Schwabing, tel. 089/3077–2150) has an indoor rink. For outdoor rinks use the **PRINZREGENTENSTADION** (Prinzregentenstr. 80, Haidhausen, tel. 089/474–808). In the west is another outdoor rink, the **EISBAHN WEST** (Agnes-Bernauer-Str. 241, Laim, tel. 8968–9007).

JOGGING

The best place to jog is the **ENGLISCHER GARTEN** (U-bahn: Münchner-Freiheit or Universität), which is 11 km (7 mi) around and has lakes and dirt and asphalt paths. You can also jog through **OLYMPIAPARK** (U-bahn: Olympiazentrum). The 500-acre park of **SCHLOSS NYMPHENBURG** (Tramway 12, Romanplatz) and the banks of the **ISAR RIVER** are also ideal for running. For a longer jog along the river, take the S-bahn to Unterföhring and pace yourself back to Münchner-Freiheit—a distance of 6½ km (4 mi).

ROWING

Rent a rowboat on the south shore of the **OLYMPIASEE** in Olympiapark or at the **KLEINHESSELOHER SEE** in the Englischer Garten.

SWIMMING

You can try swimming outdoors in the Isar River at Maria-Einsiedel, but because the river flows down from the Alps, the water is frigid even in summer. Warmer lakes near Munich are the **AMMERSEE** and the **STARNBERGERSEE**. A very relaxing experience is swimming and wellness at one of the metropolitan spas. There are pools at the **COSIMA BAD** (Englschalkingerstr. and Cosimastr., Bogenhausen), with man-made waves. The **DANTEBAD** (Dantestr. 6, Gern) has a huge lawn and is very popular in summer. The **NORDBAD** (Schleissheimerstr. 142, Schwabing) has a small, pleasant wellness section. The **MÜLLERSCHE VOLKSBAD** (Rosenheimerstr. 1, Haidhausen, tel. 2361–3434) is a grand art-nouveau building right on the Isar. Tuesday and Thursday are reserved for women only in the wellness section. And remember: if you use the saunas and steambaths in these spas, the rules say it's in your birthday suit. The **OLYMPIA-SCHWIMMHALLE** (Olympiapark, Schwabing) not only has an Olympic-size pool, but the sauna area also has a "steam cavern" as an extra delight.

TENNIS

There are about 200 outdoor courts all over Munich. Many can be booked via the sports store **SPORT SCHECK** (tel. 089/21660), which has branches around town. Prices vary from €8 to €13 an hour, depending on the time of day. Full details on tennis in Munich are available from the **BAYERISCHER TENNIS VERBAND** (Georg-Brauchle-Ring 93, Moosach, tel. 089/157–030). There are indoor and outdoor courts at Münchnerstrasse 15, in München-Unterföhring; at the corner of Drygalski-Allee and Kistlerhofstrasse, in München-Fürstenried; and at **Rothof Sportanlage** (Denningerstr., behind the Arabella and Sheraton hotels, Bogenhausen).

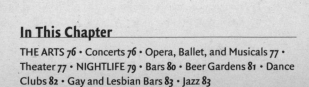

In This Chapter

nightlife and the arts

BAVARIA'S CAPITAL HAS AN ENVIABLE REPUTATION as an artistic hot spot. Various "long nights" throughout the year celebrate museum-going, books, and musical peformances. The year starts with the abandon of Fasching, the Bavarian carnival time, which begins quietly in mid-November with the crowning of the King and Queen of Fools, expands with fancy-dress balls, and ends with a great street party on Fasching Dienstag (Shrove Tuesday) in late February or early March. From spring until late fall the beer garden dictates the style and pace of Munich's nightlife. When it rains, the indoor beer halls and taverns absorb the thirstylike blotting paper.

Tickets

Some hotels will make ticket reservations, or you can book through ticket agencies in the city center, such as **MAX HIEBER KONZERTKASSE** (Liebfrauenstr. 1, City Center, tel. 089/2900–8014). Two **ZENTRALER KARTENVERKAUF** ticket kiosks are in the underground concourse at Marienplatz (City Center, tel. 089/264–620). The **ABENDZEITUNG SCHALTERHALLE** (Sendlingerstr. 10, City Center, tel. 089/267–024) is a ticket service offered by one of Munich's two rags, the *Abendzeitung*. The **RESIDENZ BÜCHERSTUBE** (Residenzstr. 1, City Center, tel. 089/220–868) only sells concert tickets. Tickets for performances at the Altes Residenztheater/Cuvilliés-Theater, Bavarian State Theater/New Residence Theater, Nationaltheater, Prinzregententheater, and Staatheater am Gartnerplatz are sold at the **CENTRAL BOX OFFICE** (Maximilianstr. 11, City Center, tel. 089/2185–1920). It's open weekdays 10–6, Saturday 10–1, and one hour before curtain time. One ticket agency, **MÜNCHEN TICKET** (tel. 089/5481–8181, www.muenchenticket.de) has a German-language Web site where tickets for most Munich theaters can be booked.

THE ARTS

Details of concerts and theater performances are listed in *Vorschau* and *Monatsprogramm*, booklets available at most hotel reception desks, newsstands, and tourist offices. Otherwise, just keep your eye open for advertising pillars and posters.

Concerts

Munich and music go together. The first Saturday in May, the **LONG NIGHT OF MUSIC** (€10, tel. 089/5481–8181) is devoted to live performances by untold numbers of groups, from heavy metal bands to medieval choirs at over 100 locations throughout the city and through the night. One ticket covers everything, including transportation on special buses between locations.

Munich's world-class concert hall, the **GASTEIG CULTURE CENTER** (Rosenheimerstr. 5, Haidhausen, tel. 089/480–980), is a lavish brick complex standing high above the Isar River, east of downtown. Its Philharmonic Hall is the permanent home of the Munich Philharmonic Orchestra. The city has three other principal orchestras, and the leading choral ensembles are the Munich Bach Choir, the Munich Motettenchor, and Musica Viva—the latter specializing in contemporary music. The choirs perform mostly in city churches.

The Bavarian Radio Symphony Orchestra performs at the **BAYERISCHER RUNDFUNK** (Rundfunkpl. 1, Maxvorstadt, tel. 089/558–080) and also at other city venues. The box office is open Monday–Thursday 9–noon and 2–4, and Friday 9–noon.

The Bavarian State Orchestra is based at the **NATIONAL THEATER** (also called the Bayerische Staatsoper; Opernpl., City Center, tel.

089/2185–1920). The Kurt Graunke Symphony Orchestra performs at the romantic art nouveau **STAATSTHEATER AM GÄRTNERPLATZ** (Gärtnerpl. 3, Isarvorstadt, tel. 089/218–51960).

HERKULESSAAL IN DER RESIDENZ (Hofgarten, City Center, tel. 089/2906–7263) is a leading orchestral and recital venue. Concerts featuring conservatory students are given free at the **HOCHSCHULE FÜR MUSIK** (Arcisstr. 12, Maxvorstadt, tel. 089/128–901).

Munich's major pop/rock concert venue is the **OLYMPIAHALLE** (U-3 Oympiazentrum stop, Georg Brauchle Ring, tel. 089/3061–3577). The box office, at the ice stadium, is open weekdays 10–6 and Saturday 10–3. You can also book by calling **München Ticket** (tel. 089/5481–8181).

Opera, Ballet, and Musicals

Munich's Bavarian State Opera Company and its ballet ensemble perform at the **NATIONALTHEATER** (Opernpl., City Center, tel. 089/2185–1920). The **STAATSTHEATER AM GÄRTNERPLATZ** (Gärtnerpl. 3, Isarvorstadt, tel. 089/218–51960) presents a less ambitious but nevertheless high-quality program of opera, ballet, operetta, and musicals.

Theater

Munich has scores of theaters and variety-show venues, although most productions will be largely impenetrable if your German is shaky. Listed here are all the better-known theaters, as well as some of the smaller and more progressive spots. Note that most theaters are closed during July and August.

ALTES RESIDENZTHEATER/CUVILLIÉS-THEATER (Max-Joseph-Pl.; entrance on Residenzstr., City Center, tel. 089/2185–1920). This is an intimate stage for compact opera productions such as Mozart's *Singspiele* and classic and contemporary plays (Arthur Miller met with great success here).

AMERIKA HAUS (America House; Karolinenpl. 3, Maxvorstadt, tel. 089/343–803). A very active American company, the American Drama Group Europe presents regular productions here.

BAYERISCHES STAATSSCHAUSPIEL/NEUES RESIDENZTHEATER (Bavarian State Theater/New Residence Theater; Max-Joseph-Pl., City Center, tel. 089/2185–1940). This is Munich's leading stage for classic playwrights such as Goethe, Schiller, Lessing, Shakespeare, and Chekhov.

DEUTSCHES THEATER (Schwanthalerstr. 13, Leopoldvorstadt, tel. 089/5523–4444). Musicals, revues, the Fasching balls, and big-band shows take place here. The box office is open weekdays noon–6 and Saturday 10–1:30.

FEIERWERK (Hansastr. 39, Westend, tel. 089/769–3600). English-language productions are regularly presented at this venue.

The Carl-Orff Saal and the Black Box theaters, in the **GASTEIG CULTURE CENTER,** occasionally present English-language plays. The box office is open weekdays 10:30–6 and Saturday 10–2.

The **KOMÖDIE IM BAYERISCHEN HOF** (Bayerischer Hof Hotel, Promenadenpl., City Center, tel. 089/292–810) offers light theatrical fare. The box office is open Monday–Saturday 11–8 and Sunday 3–8.

MÜNCHNER KAMMERSPIELE-SCHAUSPIELHAUS (Maximilianstr. 26, City Center, tel. 089/2333–7000). A city-funded rival to the nearby state-backed Staatliches Schauspiel, this theater of international renown presents the classics and new works by contemporary playwrights.

For a spectrum of good jazz, chansons, and café theater, check out the **PASINGER FABRIK** (August-Exter-Str. 1, Pasing, tel. 089/8292–9079), which also offers live music with breakfasts or late night drinks. To get there is easy: take any S-bahn out to Pasing (exit the station to the north). The box office is open Thursday–Saturday, 4:30–8:30 PM.

PRINZREGENTENTHEATER (Prinzregentenpl. 12, City Center, tel. 089/2185–2959). Munich's art-nouveau theater, an audience favorite, presents not only opera but musicals and musical gala events.

CHILDREN'S THEATER

Munich has several theaters for children. With pantomime such a strong part of the repertoire, the language problem disappears. Munich is the winter quarters of the big-top **CIRCUS KRONE** (Zirkus-Krone-Str. 1–6, Leopoldvorstadt, tel. 089/545–8000), which performs from Christmas until the end of March. The **MÜNCHNER MARIONETTENTHEATER** (Blumenstr. 32, City Center, tel. 089/265–712) lets its puppets chew on highbrow material, notably works of Carl Orff. The **MÜNCHNER THEATER FÜR KINDER** (Dachauerstr. 46, Neuhausen, tel. 089/595–454) will keep the young ones happy with fairy tales and traditional pieces such as *Pinocchio*. The puppet shows at **OTTO BILLE'S MARIONETTENBÜHNE** (Bereiterangerstr. 15, Au, tel. 089/150–2168) are for young children. The **SCHAUBURG THEATER DER JUGEND** (Franz-Joseph-Str. 47, Schwabing, tel. 089/2333–7171) appeals to older youth, including adults.

NIGHTLIFE

Beer gardens and most beer halls close at midnight, but there's no need to go home to bed: some bars and nightclubs are open until 6 AM. A word of caution about some of those bars: most are run honestly, and prices are only slightly higher than normal, but a few may intentionally overcharge. The seedier ones are near the main train station. Stick to beer or wine if you can, and pay as you go.

Clubs, discos and the like can be a bit of a problem in Munich: the bouncers outside are for the most part there to add to the often specious exclusivity of the inside. Bouncers are usually rude, crude, and somewhat thick, but as such have achieved dubious notoriety throughout Germany. However they are in charge of picking who is "in" and who is "out," and there's no use trying to warm up to them.

Bars

On fashionable Maximilianstrasse, **O'REILLY'S IRISH CELLAR PUB** (Maximilianstr. 29, City Center, tel. 089/293–311) offers escape from the German bar scene as it pours genuine Irish Guinness. The bartenders are busy shaking cocktails at **SCHUMANN'S** (Maximilianstr. 36, City Center, tel. 089/229–060) after the curtain comes down at the nearby opera house (the bar is closed on Saturday). The **KEMPINSKI VIER JAHRESZEITEN** (Maximilianstr. 17, City Center, tel. 089/21250) offers piano music until 9 and then dancing to recorded music or a small combo.

Exotic cocktails are the specialty of **TRADER VIC'S** (Promenadenpl. 4, City Center, tel. 089/226–192), a smart cellar bar in the Hotel Bayerischer Hof. The bar is particularly popular among out-of-town visitors and attracts quite a few Americans. The Bayerischer Hof's **NIGHT CLUB** (Promenadepl. 2–6, City Center, tel. 089/212–0994) has live music, a small dance floor, and a very lively bar (avoid the poorly made mixed drinks). Jazz groups perform regularly there, too. Great cocktails and Irish-German black and tans (Guinness and strong German beer) are made to the sounds of live jazz at the English nautical-style **PUSSER'S NEW YORK BAR** (Falkenturmstr. 9, City Center, tel. 089/220–500). The pricey sandwiches such as the pastrami are about the only "New York" in Pussers.

Wait until after midnight before venturing into the **ALTER SIMPL** (Türkenstr. 57, Schwabing, tel. 089/272–3083), where a sparkling crowd enlivens the cold glass-and-steel interior. **EISBACH** (Marstallstr. 3, Lehel, tel. 089/2280–1680) occupies a corner of the Max Planck Institute building opposite the Bavarian Parliament. The bar is among Munich's longest and is overlooked by a mezzanine restaurant area where you can choose from a limited but ambitious menu. Outdoor tables nestle in the expansive shade of huge parasols. The nearby Eisbach Brook, which gives the bar its name, tinkles away like ice in the glass. Designed to the last corner in modern style, **SCALAR** (Seitzstr. 12, Lehel, tel. 089/ 2157–9636) attracts a fairly mixed crowd of well-designed people. Its cellar is home to the Blue Oyster Club, where dancing is encouraged.

Beer Gardens

Each person in Munich has at least one favorite beer garden, so you're in good hands if you ask someone to point you in the right direction. You do not need to reserve, that is not the point of the beer garden. No need to phone either: if the weather says yes, then go. Note, however, that Munich has very strict noise laws, so beer gardens tend to close around 11. The two big and famous beer gardens are in the Englischer Garten. The **BIERGARTEN AM CHINESISCHEN TURM** (tel. 089/383–8730) is at the five-story Chinese Tower in the Englisher Garten. The Englischer Garten's smaller beer garden, **HIRSCHAU** (tel. 089/369–945), has minigolf to test your skills after a few beers. It's about 10 minutes north of the Kleinhesselohersee. The **SEEHAUS IM ENGLISCHEN GARTEN** (tel. 089/381–6130) is on the banks of the artificial lake Kleinhesselohersee, where all of Munich converges on hot summer days (bus line 44, exit at Osterwaldstrasse; you can't miss it). Surprisingly large and green for a place so centrally located is the **HOFBRÄUKELLER** (Innere Wiener Str. 19, tramway 18 to Wiener-Pl. or U-bahn 4 or 5 to Max-Weber-Pl., Haidhausen, tel. 089/459–9250), which is a beer relative of the Hofbräuhaus. Some evenings you can move into the spacious cellar for some live jazz. Out in the district of Laim is the huge **KÖNIGLICHER HIRSCHGARTEN** (tel. 089/172–591), where the crowd is somewhat more blue-collar and foreign. To get there take any S-bahn toward Pasing, exit at Laim, walk down Wotanstrasse, take a right on Winifriedstrasse and then a left into De-la-Paz-Strasse. The crowd at the **TAXISGARTEN** (tel. 089/

156–827) in the Gern district (U-bahn Gern, Line 1 toward "Westfriedhof") is more white collar–oriented and tame, hence less chance of communicating with the natives, as it were, but the food is excellent and while parents refresh themselves, the children can enjoy a nice playground.

Dance Clubs

Schwabing claims more than a dozen dance clubs and live music venues between its central boulevard, Leopoldstrasse, and the area around its central square, the Münchner-Freiheit. Two streets—Feilitzstrasse and Occamstrasse—are lined with clubs, discos, and pubs. Haidhausen is Munich's other "in" area. A former factory hosts the city's largest rave scene: the **KUNSTPARK OST** (Grafingerstr. 6, Haidhausen, S-bahn, bus, or to Ostbahnhof, tel. 089/4900–2928). The venue has no fewer than 17 "entertainment areas," including a Latin dance club among others, bars, and a huge slot-machine and computer-game hall. Kunstpark Ost may be migrating toward the north of Munich. **MUFFATHALLE**'s (Rosenheimerstr. 1, behind the Müllersche Volksbad, Haidhausen, tel. 4587–5010) burnt orange programs with dates in a purple column are usually posted on advertising pillars. Hodgepodge is the only way to describe the events, but the atmosphere is relaxed, young, and nonchalant. The **SKYLINE** (Münchner-Freiheit, Schwabing, tel. 089/333–131) is at the top of the Hertie department store, which towers above a busy square. Bordering the Englisher Garten, **P 1** (Prinzregentenstr., on west side of Haus der Kunst, Lehel, tel. 089/294–252) is allegedly the trendiest club in town; find out for yourself, and good luck making it past the bouncer. The **PARK-CAFÉ** (Sophienstr. 7, Maxvorstadt, tel. 089/598–313) is one of those fashionable places where you'll have to talk yourself past the doorman to join the chic crowds inside.

The **FEIERWERK** (Hansastr. 39, Westend, tel. 089/769–3600) has that oh-so-attractive ramshackle old factory look to it, but it is a genuine institution in the musical scene. Many local bands were launched to fame—and back—here. The big FEST festival in July is one of the city's better alternatives in the night scene. **NACHTWERK** (Landsbergerstr. 185, Westend, tel. 089/570–7390), in a converted factory, blasts out a range of sounds from punk to avant-garde nightly between 8 PM and 4 AM. Live bands also perform here regularly. The real ravers ride the S-bahn to Munich's Franz-Josef-Strauss Airport, alighting at the Besucherpark station for techno and other beats until dawn at **NIGHT FLIGHT** (tel. 089/9759–7999).

Gay and Lesbian Bars

Munich's growing gay scene stretches between Sendlingertorplatz and Isartorplatz. For an overview check www.munich-cruising.de. The **NIL** (Hans-Sachs-Str. 2, Isarvorstadt, tel. 089/265–545) is famous for its decent prices and its schnitzel. The **FORTUNA** (Maximilianstr. 5, Isarvorstadt, tel. 089/554–070) is more than just a bar and disco for women, it's also an events venue and organizer (skiing excursions, rafting on the Isar, for example). **FREDS PUB** (Reisingerstr. 15, Isarvorstadt, tel. 089/260–22809) shows gay movies on a large screen for the edification of its patrons. The upscale **MORIZZ** (Klenzestr. 43, Isarvorstadt, tel. 089/201–6776) fills with a somewhat ritzy crowd. The **OCHSENGARTEN** (Müllerstr. 47, Isarvorstadt, tel. 089/266–446) is Munich's leather bar. **OLD MRS. HENDERSON** (Rumfordstr. 2, Isarvorstadt, tel. 089/263–469) puts on the city's best transvestite cabaret for a mixed crowd and has various other events.

Jazz

Munich likes to think it's Germany's jazz capital, and some beer gardens have taken to replacing their brass bands with funky combos. Jazz musicians sometimes accompany Sunday brunch at pubs, too. One top club is the tiny **MR. B'S** (Herzog-Heinrich-Str. 38, Isarvorstadt, tel. 089/534–901), run by New Yorker Alex Best, who also mixes great cocktails, and unlike so many

Not a Night Owl?

You can learn a lot about a place if you take its pulse after dark. So even if you're the original early-to-bed type, there's every reason to vary your routine when you're away from home.

EXPERIENCE THE FAMILIAR IN A NEW PLACE Whether your thing is going to the movies or going to concerts, it's always different away from home. In clubs, new faces and new sounds add up to a different scene. Or you may catch movies you'd never see at home.

TRY SOMETHING NEW Do something you've never done before. It's another way to dip into the local scene. A simple suggestion: Go out later than usual—go dancing late and finish up with breakfast at dawn.

DO SOMETHING OFFBEAT Look into lectures and readings as well as author appearances in book stores. You may even meet your favorite novelist.

EXPLORE A DAYTIME NEIGHBORHOOD AT NIGHT Take a nighttime walk through an explorable area you've already seen by day. You'll get a whole different view of it.

ASK AROUND If you strike up a conversation with like-minded people during the course of your day, ask them about their favorite spots. Your hotel concierge is another resource.

DON'T WING IT As soon as you've nailed down your travel dates, look into local publications or surf the Net to see what's on the calendar while you're in town. Look for hot regional acts, dance and theater, big-name performing artists, expositions, and sporting events. Then call or click to order tickets.

CHECK OUT THE NEIGHBORHOOD Whenever you don't know the neighborhood you'll be visiting, review safety issues with people in your hotel. What's the transportation situation? Can you walk there, or do you need a cab? Is there anything else you need to know?

CASH OR CREDIT? Know before you go. It's always fun to be surprised—but not when you can't cover your check.

barkeeps, usually sports a welcoming smile on his face. The **UNTERFAHRT** (Einsteinstr. 42, Haidhausen, tel. 089/448–2794) is the place for the serious jazzologist, though hip-hop is making heavy inroads into the scene. A haunt with nondescript furnishings rather than chic dilapidation is **NACHTCAFÉ** (Maximilianpl. 5, City Center, tel. 089/595–900). Food (costly) is served all night, and there's no dancing. Sunday is set aside for jazz at **WALDWIRTSCHAFT GROSSHESSELOHE** (Georg-Kalb-Str. 3, Grosshesselohe, tel. 089/795–088) in a southern suburb. If it's a nice day, the excursion is worth it.

In This Chapter

where to stay

THOUGH MUNICH HAS A VAST NUMBER OF HOTELS in all price ranges, many are fully booked year-round; this is a major trade and convention city as well as a prime tourist destination. If you're visiting during Mode Wochen (Fashion Weeks), in March and September, or during Oktoberfest at the end of September, make reservations at least six months in advance.

Some of the large, very expensive hotels that cater to expense-account business travelers have very attractive weekend discount rates—sometimes as much as 50% below normal prices. Conversely, regular rates can go up during big trade fairs.

Munich's two tourist information offices—at the main railway station and in the city center (Marienplatz, in the Rathaus)—make hotel bookings. Telephone lines are usually busy, so your best bet is to visit one of the offices personally.

Prices

CATEGORY	COST*
$$$$	over €225
$$$	€150–€225
$$	€75–€150
$	under €75

*All prices are for two people in a double room, including tax and service.

munich lodging

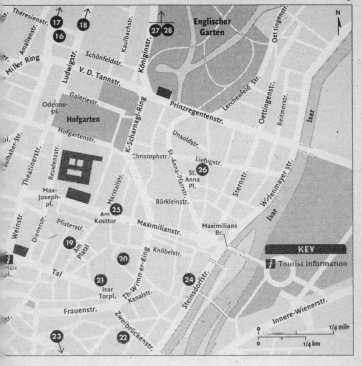

Kurpfalz, 9
Mayer, 11
Olympic, 14
Park–Hotel
Theresienhöhe, 7
Platzl, 19
Rotkreuzplatz, 1
Torbräu, 21

CITY CENTER

$$$$ BAYERISCHER HOF. Germany's most respected family-owned hotel, the Bayerischer Hof began its rich history by hosting Ludwig I's guests. Public rooms are grandly laid out with marble, antiques, and oil paintings. Laura Ashley–decorated rooms look out to the city's skyline of towers. Rooms facing the interior courtyard are the least expensive and begin at €254. Nightlife is built into the hotel, with Trader Vic's bar and dancing at the Night Club. *Promenadepl. 2–6, City Center D–80333, tel. 089/21200, fax 089/212–0906, www.bayerischerhof.de. 306 rooms, 45 suites. 3 restaurants, cable TV with movies and video games, pool, hair salon, massage, sauna, bar, nightclub, Internet, meeting rooms, parking (fee), some pets allowed (fee), no-smoking rooms. AE, DC, MC, V.*

$$$$ KEMPINSKI HOTEL VIER JAHRESZEITEN MÜNCHEN. The Four ★ Seasons has been playing host to the world's wealthy and titled for more than a century. It has an unbeatable location on Maximilianstrasse, Munich's premier shopping street, only a few minutes' walk from the heart of the city. Elegance and luxury set the tone throughout; many rooms have handsome antique pieces. The Bistro Eck is on the main floor, and the Theater bar/restaurant is in the cellar. The afternoon tea in the poshly decorated foyer is a special treat. *Maximilianstr. 17, City Center D–80539, tel. 089/21250; 516/794–2670 for Kempinski Reservation Service, fax 089/2125–2000, www.Kempinski-Vierjahreszeiten.de. 268 rooms, 48 suites. 2 restaurants, cable TV with movies, pool, health club, massage, sauna, piano bar, meeting rooms, car rental, parking (fee), some pets allowed (fee), no-smoking rooms. AE, DC, MC, V.*

$$$–$$$$ PLATZL. The Platzl, which is a privately owned enterprise, has won awards and wide recognition for its ecologically aware management. It stands in the historic heart of Munich, near the famous Hofbräuhaus beer hall and a couple of minutes' walk from Marienplatz and many other landmarks. Its Pfistermühle restaurant, with 16th-century vaulting, is one of the area's oldest and most historic establishments. *Sparkassenstr. 10, City Center*

D–80331, tel. 089/237–030; 800/448–8355 in the U.S., fax 089/2370–3800, www.platzl.de. 167 rooms. Restaurant, cable TV with movies, gym, sauna, steam room, bar, parking (fee), some pets allowed (fee); no a/c in some rooms, no-smoking rooms. AE, DC, MC, V.

$$$–$$$$ **TORBRÄU.** In this snug hotel you'll sleep under the shadow of one of Munich's ancient city gates—the 14th-century Isartor. The location is excellent as it's midway between the Marienplatz and the Deutsches Museum (and around the corner from the Hofbräuhaus). The hotel has been run by the same family for more than a century. Comfortable rooms are decorated in a plush and ornate Italian style. Its Italian restaurant, *La Famiglia*, is one of the best in the area. Tal 41, City Center D–80331, tel. 089/242–340, fax 089/234–235, www.torbraeu.de. 83 rooms, 3 suites. Restaurant, café, cable TV, in-room data ports, gym, sauna, bowling, meeting rooms, some pets allowed (fee); no a/c in some rooms, no-smoking rooms. AE, MC, V.

$$ **OLYMPIC.** The English-style entrance lobby, with its leather easy chairs and mahogany fittings, is an attractive introduction to this friendly small hotel, a beautifully converted turn-of-the-20th-century mansion, amid the bars and boutiques of the colorful district between Sendlinger Tor and Isartor. Most of the rooms look out over a quiet interior courtyard. Do not expect constant and fawning care: the style of the hotel is casual, the idea is to make the guest feel really at home. Hans-Sachs-Str. 4, City Center D–80469, tel. 089/231–890, fax 089/2318–9199. 38 rooms, 3 apartments. Cable TV, in-room data ports, parking (fee), some pets allowed (fee); no a/c. AE, DC, MC, V.

ISARVORSTADT

$$$–$$$$ **ADMIRAL.** The small, privately owned Admiral enjoys a quiet side-
★ street location and its own garden, close to the Isar River and Deutsches Museum. Many of the simply furnished and warmly decorated bedrooms have a balcony overlooking the garden. Bowls of fresh fruit are part of the friendly welcome awaiting guests. The breakfast buffet is a dream, complete with homemade jams, in-

season strawberries, and Italian and French delicacies. *Kohlstr. 9, Isarvorstadt D–80469, tel. 089/216–350, fax 089/293–674, www. hotel-admiral.de. 33 rooms. Cable TV, in-room data ports, bar, parking (fee), some pets allowed; no a/c, no-smoking rooms. AE, DC, MC, V.*

$$–$$$ ADVOKAT. Owner Kevin Voigt designed much of his hotel's exquisite furniture, which was then made by Italian craftsmen. The Italian touch is everywhere, from the sleek, minimalist lines of the bedroom furniture and fittings to the choice prints and modern Florentine mirrors on the walls. If you value modern taste over plush luxury, this is the hotel for you. *Baaderstr. 1, Isarvorstadt D–80469, tel. 089/216–310, fax 089/216–3190, www.hotel-advokat.de. 50 rooms. Cable TV, in-room data ports, parking (fee), some pets allowed; no a/c, no-smoking rooms AE, DC, MC, V.*

$ HOTEL-PENSION SCHMELLERGARTEN. ★ This genuine family business will make you feel right at home, and is very popular with young budget travelers. The little place is on a quiet street just off Lindwurmstrasse, a few minutes' walk from the Theresienwiese (Oktoberfest). The Poccistrasse subway station is around the corner to take you into the center of town. *Schmellerstr. 20, Isarvorstadt D–80337, tel. 089/773–157, fax 089/725–6886. 14 rooms. Some pets allowed; no a/c. No credit cards.*

MAXVORSTADT

$$–$$$$ CARLTON. This is a favorite of many diplomats, professors, and business executives on tight schedules and in need of a top-notch place to stay: a small, elegant, discreet hotel on a quiet side street in the best area of downtown Munich. Some of the liveliest student bars and restaurants are nearby, as are galleries, museums, and movie theaters. Rooms are on the small side but comfortable. A glass of champagne is included in the complimentary buffet breakfast. *Fürstenstr. 12, Maxvorstadt D–80333, tel. 089/282–061, fax 089/284–391. 50 rooms. Cable TV with movies, sauna, some pets allowed (fee), no-smoking rooms. AE, DC, MC, V.*

$$ ERZGIESSEREI EUROPE. Its location on a quiet, residential section of the city is hardly a drawback, because the nearby subway whisks you in five minutes to Karlsplatz, convenient to the pedestrian shopping area and the main railway station. Rooms in this attractive, modern hotel are particularly bright, decorated in soft pastels with good reproductions on the walls. The cobblestone garden café is a haven of peace. *Erzgiessereistr. 15, Maxvorstadt D–80335, tel. 089/126–820, fax 089/123–6198, www. top-hotels.de/erzeurope. 105 rooms, 1 suite. Restaurant, café, cable TV with movies, in-room data ports, bar, parking (fee), some pets allowed (fee); no a/c, no-smoking rooms. AE, DC, MC, V.*

$ HOTEL PENSION AM SIEGESTOR. ★ This modest but very appealing pension takes up three floors of a fin-de-siècle mansion between the Siegestor monument, on Leopoldstrasse, and the university. An ancient wood-paneled, glass-door elevator brings you to the fourth-floor reception desk. Most of the simply furnished rooms face the impressive Arts Academy across the street. Rooms on the fifth floor are particularly cozy, tucked up under the eaves. *Akademiestr. 5, Maxvorstadt D–80799, tel. 089/399–550 or 089/399–551, fax 089/343–050. 20 rooms. No room phones, no TV in some rooms. No credit cards.*

SCHWABING

$$–$$$ BIEDERSTEIN. The hotel is not the prettiest from the outside—a modern, uninspired block—but it seems to want to fit into its old Schwabing surroundings. At the rim of the Englischer Garten, the Biederstein has many advantages: peace and quiet; excellent service; and comfortable, well-appointed rooms that were carefully renovated. Guests are requested to smoke on the balconies, not inside. *Keferstr. 18, Schwabing D–80335, tel. 089/389–9970, fax 089/3899–97389. 34 rooms, 7 suites. Cable TV, bar, free parking, some pets allowed (fee); no a/c. AE, DC, MC, V.*

$$ GÄSTEHAUS AM ENGLISCHEN GARTEN. ★ Reserve well in advance for a room at this popular converted water mill, more than 200 years old, adjoining the Englischer Garten. The hotel is only a five-minute walk from the bars, shops, and restaurants of Schwabing. Be sure to ask for one of the 12 nostalgically old-fashioned rooms in the main building; a modern annex down the road has 13 apartments, all with cooking facilities. In summer breakfast is served on the terrace of the main house, which has a garden on an island in the old millrace. *Liebergesellstr. 8, Schwabing D–80802, tel. 089/383–9410, fax 089/3839–4133. 12 rooms, 6 with bath or shower; 13 apartments. Cable TV, free parking, some pets allowed (fee); no a/c. AE, DC, MC, V.*

LEOPOLDVORSTADT

$$$–$$$$ EDEN-HOTEL WOLFF. Chandeliers and dark-wood paneling in the public rooms contribute to the old-fashioned elegance of this downtown favorite. It's directly across the street from the train station and near the Theresienwiese fairgrounds. The rooms come with plush comforts, and most are spacious. You can dine on excellent Bavarian specialties in the intimate Zirbelstube restaurant. *Arnulfstr. 4, Leopoldvorstadt D–80335, tel. 089/551–150, fax 089/5511–5555, www.ehw.de. 209 rooms, 7 suites. Restaurant, café, bar, cable TV with movies, gym, Internet, meeting rooms, parking (fee), some pets allowed (fee); no a/c in some rooms. AE, DC, MC, V.*

$$–$$$ BRACK. Oktoberfest revelers value the Brack's proximity to the beer festival grounds, and its location—on a busy, tree-lined thoroughfare just south of the center—is handy for city attractions. Rooms are furnished in light, friendly veneers and are soundproof (a useful feature during Oktoberfest) and have amenities such as hair dryers and cable TV. The buffet breakfast will set you up for the day. *Lindwurmstr. 153, Leopoldvorstadt D–80337, tel. 089/747–2550, fax 089/7472–5599, www.hotel-brack.de. 50 rooms. Cable TV with movies, free parking; no a/c. AE, DC, MC, V.*

$$–$$$ HOTEL AMBA. Don't waste a second with additional travel. The Amba, which is right next to the train station, has clean, bright rooms, good service, no expensive frills, and everything you need to plug and play as it were. No sooner have you enjoyed a solid breakfast at the buffet (with sparkling wine), than you'll be out on the town visiting the nearby sights on foot. *Arnulfstr. 20, Leopoldvorstadt D–80636, tel. 089/545–140, fax 089/5451–1555, www.hotel-amba.de. 86 rooms. Cable TV with movies, some pets allowed (fee); no a/c, no-smoking rooms. AE, DC, MC, V.*

$$ **HOTEL MIRABELL.** This family-run hotel is used to American
★ tourists who appreciate the friendly atmosphere, central location (between the main railway station and the Oktoberfest fairgrounds), and reasonable room rates. Three apartments are for small groups or families. All rooms have TVs and phones, and are furnished in modern light woods and bright prints. Breakfast is the only meal served, but snacks can be ordered at the bar. Prices are much higher during trade fairs and Oktoberfest. *Landwehrstr. 42 (entrance on Goethestr.), Leopoldvorstadt D–80336, tel. 089/549–1740, fax 089/550–3701. 65 rooms, 3 apartments. Cable TV with movies, in-room data ports, bar, some pets allowed (fee), no-smoking rooms. AE, MC, V.*

$–$$ **HOTEL-PENSION MARIANDL.** The American armed forces commandeered this turn-of-the-20th-century neo-Gothic mansion in May 1945 and established Munich's first postwar nightclub, the Femina, on the ground floor (now the charming café-restaurant, Cafe am Beethovenplatz). Most rooms are mansion size, with high ceilings and large windows overlooking a leafy avenue. The Oktoberfest grounds and the main railway station are both a 10-minute walk away. *Goethestr. 51, Leopoldvorstadt D–80336, tel. 089/534–108, fax 089/5440–4396. 28 rooms. Restaurant, some pets allowed; no a/c, no room phones, no TVs. AE, DC, MC, V.*

$ **KURPFALZ.** Guests have praised the friendly welcome and service they receive at this centrally placed and affordable lodging. Rooms are comfortable, if furnished in a manner only slightly better than functional, and all are equipped with satellite TV. Breakfast is included. The main train station and Oktoberfest grounds are both within a 10-minute walk, and the area is rich in restaurants, bars, and movie theaters. *Schwantalerstr. 121, Leopoldvorstadt D–80339, tel. 089/540–986, fax 089/5409–8811. 44 rooms with shower.*

In-room data ports, cable TV, bar, some pets allowed; no a/c, no-smoking rooms. AE, MC, V.

LEHEL

$$–$$$ ADRIA. This modern, comfortable hotel is ideally set in the upmarket area of Lehel, in the middle of Munich's museum quarter. Rooms are large and tastefully decorated, with old prints on the pale-pink walls, Oriental rugs on the floors, and flowers beside the double beds. A spectacular breakfast buffet (including a glass of sparkling wine) is included in the room rate. There's no hotel restaurant, but the area is rich in good restaurants, bistros, and bars. *Liebigstr. 8a, Lehel D–80538, tel. 089/242–1170, fax 089/242–117999, www. adria-muenchen.de. 43 rooms. Cable TV, in-room data ports, some pets allowed (fee); no a/c, no-smoking rooms. AE, MC, V.*

$$ HOTEL CONCORDE. The centrally located Concorde wants to do its bit toward relieving traffic congestion, so guests who arrive from the airport on the S-bahn can exchange their ticket at the reception desk for a welcome champagne or cocktail. The nearest S-bahn station (Isartor) is only a two-minute walk away. Rooms are done in pastel tones and light woods. Fresh flowers and bright prints add a colorful touch. A large breakfast buffet is served in its stylish, mirrored Salon Margarita. *Herrnstr. 38, Lehel D–80539, tel. 089/224–515, fax 089/228–3282. 67 rooms, 4 suites. Cable TV, in-room data ports, parking (fee), some pets allowed (fee), no-smoking rooms. AE, DC, MC, V.*

$ HOTEL-PENSION BECK. American and British guests receive a
★ particularly warm welcome from the Anglophile owner of the rambling, friendly Beck (she and her pet canary are a regular presence). Bright carpeting, with matching pinewood furniture, gives rooms a cheerful touch. The pension has no elevator, but does have a prime location convenient to the museums on Prinzregentenstrasse and to the Englischer Garten. *Thierschstr.*

36, Lehel D–80538, tel. 089/220–708 or 089/225–768, fax 089/220–925, www.bst-online.de/pension.beck. 44 rooms, 7 with shower. cable TV, some in-room data ports, some pets allowed; no a/c. MC, V.

NYMPHENBURG

$$ KRIEMHILD. If you're traveling with children, you'll appreciate this welcoming, family-run pension in a western suburb near parks and gardens. It's a 10-minute walk from Schloss Nymphenburg and around the corner from the Hirschgarten Park, site of one of the city's best beer gardens. The tram ride (No. 16 or 17 to Kriemhildenstrasse stop) from the train station is 10 minutes. The buffet breakfast is included in the rate. *Guntherstr. 16, Nymphenburg D–80639, tel. 089/171–1170, fax 089/1711–1755, www.kriemhild.de. 18 rooms. Cable TV, in-room data ports, bar, free parking, some pets allowed; no a/c. AE, MC, V.*

OUTER MUNICH

$$–$$$$ ARABELLASHERATON GRAND HOTEL. The building itself may raise a few eyebrows. It stands on a slight elevation and is not the most shapely on the Munich skyline. What goes on inside is sheer five-star luxury for the leisure or business traveler. Guests are greeted with a glass of champagne, snacks and drinks are available round the clock in the Towers Lounge. The excellent restaurant Ente vom Lehel has come to roost here, as well. And if you need a special Bavarian flavor to your stay, then book one of the 60 "Bavarian rooms." *Arabellastr. 5, Bogenhausen D–81925, tel. 089/92640, fax 089/9264–8699, www.arabellasheraton.de. 644 rooms, 31 suites. 2 restaurants, cable TV with movies, pool, sauna, steam room, hair salon, bars, Internet, business services, meeting rooms, parking, some pets allowed (fee), no-smoking rooms. AE, DC, MC, V.*

$$$ PARK-HOTEL THERESIENHÖHE. The Park-Hotel claims that none of its rooms are less than 400 square ft. Suites are larger than many luxury apartments, and some of them come with small kitchens.

Hotel How-Tos

Where you stay does make a difference. Do you prefer a modern high-rise or an intimate B&B? A center-city location or the quiet suburbs? What facilities do you want? Sort through your priorities, then price it all out.

HOW TO GET A DEAL After you've chosen a likely candidate or two, phone them directly and price a room for your travel dates. Then call the hotel's toll-free number and ask the same questions. Also try consolidators and hotel-room discounters. You won't hear the same rates twice. On the spot, make a reservation as soon as you are quoted a price you want to pay.

PROMISES, PROMISES If you have special requests, make them when you reserve. Get written confirmation of any promises.

SETTLE IN Upon arriving, make sure everything works—lights and lamps, TV and radio, sink, tub, shower, and anything else that matters. Report any problems immediately. And don't wait until you need extra pillows or blankets or an ironing board to call housekeeping. Also check out the fire emergency instructions. Know where to find the fire exits, and make sure your companions do, too.

IF YOU NEED TO COMPLAIN Be polite but firm. Explain the problem to the person in charge. Suggest a course of action. If you aren't satisfied, repeat your requests to the manager. Document everything: Take pictures and keep a written record of who you've spoken with, when, and what was said. Contact your travel agent, if he made the reservations.

KNOW THE SCORE When you go out, take your hotel's business cards (one for everyone in your party). If you have extras, you can give them out to new acquaintances who want to call you.

TIP UP FRONT For special services, a tip or partial tip in advance can work wonders.

USE ALL THE HOTEL RESOURCES A concierge can make difficult things easy. But a desk clerk, bellhop, or other hotel employee who's friendly, smart, and ambitious can often steer you straight as well. A gratuity is in order if the advice is helpful.

The sleek, modern rooms are mostly decorated with light woods and pastel-color fabrics and carpeting; larger rooms and suites get a lot of light, thanks to the floor-to-ceiling windows. Families are particularly welcome, and a baby-sitting service is provided. There's no in-house restaurant, but you can order in. *Parkstr. 31, Westend D–80339, tel. 089/519–950, fax 089/5199–5420. 35 rooms. Cable TV, some in-room data ports, bar, baby-sitting, pets allowed; no a/c, no-smoking rooms. AE, DC, MC, V.*

$$ JAGDSCHLOSS. This century-old hunting lodge in Munich's leafy Obermenzing suburb is a delightful hotel. The rustic look has been retained, with lots of original woodwork and white stucco. Many of the comfortable pastel-tone bedrooms have wooden balconies with flower boxes bursting with color. In the beamed restaurant or sheltered beer garden you'll be served Bavarian specialties by a staff dressed in traditional lederhosen (shorts in summer, breeches in winter). *Alte Allee 21, D–81245, München-Obermenzing, tel. 089/820–820, fax 089/8208–2100, www.weber-gastronomie.de. 22 rooms, 1 suite. Restaurant, cable TV, beer garden, playground, free parking, some pets allowed; no a/c. MC, V.*

$$ MAYER. If you are willing to sacrifice location for good value, head for this family-run hotel 25 minutes by suburban train from the Hauptbahnhof. The Mayer's first-class comforts and facilities cost about half of what you'd pay at similar lodgings in town. It is furnished in Bavarian country-rustic style—lots of pine and green and red, and check fabrics. The Mayer is a 10-minute walk or a short taxi ride from Germering station on the S-5 line, eight stops west of the Hauptbahnhof. *Augsburgerstr. 45, D–82110, Germering, tel. 089/844–071, fax 089/844–094, www.hotel-mayer.de. 65 rooms. Restaurant, cable TV, in-room data ports, pool, some pets allowed (fee), no-smoking rooms. AE, DC, MC, V.*

$$ ROTKREUZPLATZ. This small, family-run business on lively Rotkreuzplatz is five minutes by subway (U-1 and U-7) from the main train station. Breakfast in the neighboring café is included in the price. There are no grand amenities, but a pleasant stay is

Your Checklist for a Perfect Journey

WAY AHEAD
- Devise a trip budget.

- Write down the five things you want most from this trip. Keep this list handy before and during your trip.

- Make plane or train reservations. Book lodging and rental cars.

- Arrange for pet care.

- Check your passport. Apply for a new one if necessary.

- Photocopy important documents and store in a safe place.

A MONTH BEFORE
- Make restaurant reservations and buy theater and concert tickets. Visit fodors.com for links to local events.

- Familiarize yourself with the local language or lingo.

TWO WEEKS BEFORE
- Replenish your supply of medications.

- Create your itinerary.

- Enjoy a book or movie set in your destination to get you in the mood.

- Develop a packing list. Shop for missing essentials. Repair and launder or dry-clean your clothes.

A WEEK BEFORE
- Stop newspaper deliveries. Pay bills.

- Acquire traveler's checks.

- Stock up on film.

- Label your luggage.

- Finalize your packing list— take less than you think you need.

- Create a toiletries kit filled with travel-size essentials.

- Get lots of sleep. Don't get sick before your trip.

A DAY BEFORE
- Drink plenty of water.

- Check your travel documents.

- Get packing!

DURING YOUR TRIP
- Keep a journal/scrapbook.

- Spend time with locals.

- Take time to explore. Don't plan too much.

guaranteed. You can watch over one of Munich's most original squares, where people from all walks of life meet around a modern fountain. *Rotkreuzpl. 2, Neuhausen D–80634, tel. 089/139–9080, fax 089/166–469. 56 rooms. Cable TV, in-room data ports, parking, pets allowed, no-smoking rooms. AE, DC, MC, V.*

In This Chapter

side trips

MUNICH'S EXCELLENT SUBURBAN RAILWAY NETWORK, the S-bahn, brings several quaint towns and attractive rural areas within easy reach for a day's excursion. The two nearest lakes, the Starnbergersee and the Ammersee, are popular year-round. Dachau attracts overseas visitors, mostly because of its concentration-camp memorial site, but it's a picturesque and historic town in its own right. Landshut, north of Munich, is way off the tourist track, but if it were the same distance south of Munich in the foothills, this jewel of a Bavarian market town would be overrun. Wasserburg am Inn is held in the narrow embrace of the Inn River, and it's easily incorporated into an excursion to the nearby lake, Chiemsee, where King Ludwig built a sumptuous island palace, Schloss Herrenchiemsee. All these destinations have a wide selection of restaurants and hotels, and you can bring a bike on any S-bahn train. German railways, DB, often has weekend specials during which a family or group of five can travel for as little as €17.50 during certain times. (Inquire at the main train station for the "Wochenendticket.")

STARNBERGERSEE
20 km (12 mi) southwest of Munich.

The Starnbergersee was one of Europe's first pleasure grounds. Royal coaches were already trundling out from Munich to the lake's wooded shores in the 17th century; in 1663 Elector Ferdinand Maria threw a shipboard party at which 500 guests wined and dined as 100 oarsmen propelled them around the lake. Today pleasure steamers provide a taste of such luxury to

Dachau

TO LANDSHUT

A92

A99

München

A96

A8

Stegen
Inning
Unterhaching
Pullach
Ottobrunn
Kirchseeon
Ebers
Grafi
Grünwald
Taufkchn
Hohenbrunn
Oberhaching
Herrsching
Starnberg
Berg
Feldkirchen
Ammersee
Westerhan
Diessen
Wolfratshausen
Bruc
Tutzing
Geretsried
Holzkirchen
Starnbergersee
TO
LUDWIG'S
CASTLE
Bad Tölz
Gmund
472
Schlierse
Blomberg
Tegernsee
Rottach-Egern
Benediktbeuern
Bad Wiessee
Spitzingse
Murnau
Wallberg
Lenggries
Kochelsee
Kochel
Oberammergau
Walchensee
A U S T R I A
Linderhof
Ettal
Zugspitze
Garmisch-Partenkirchen
Jenbach
Mittenwald
Schwaz

Isar

A95

Ebersburg

Grafing

Wasserburg

Trostberg

Laufen

20

15

304

Traunreut

Stock

Chiemsee

Teisendorf

Freilassing

Salzburg

erham

Fraueninsel

Traunstein

Ainring

Bruckmühl

Rosenheim

A8

Rottau

Ruhpolding

Wals

Bernau

Grassau

305

Bad Reichenhall

Aschau

Marquartstein

Hallein

nliersee

Rossholzen

Unterwössen

29

A12

Oberwössen

105

gern

Reit im Winkl

Obersalzberg

ngsee

Tatzelwurm

Berchtesgaden

305

Bayrischzell

Königssee

Kufstein

St. Johann

Obersee

Inn

Kitzbühel

Saalfelden

ach

Wörgl

Zell
am See

z

N

0   20 miles

0   30 km

the masses. The lake is still lined with the small baroque palaces of Bavaria's aristocracy, but their owners now share the lakeside with public parks, beaches, and boatyards. The Starnbergersee is one of Bavaria's largest lakes—20 km (12 mi) long and 5 km (3 mi) wide—so there's plenty of room for swimmers, sailors, and windsurfers. The water is of drinking quality (as with most Bavarian lakes), a testimony to stringent environmental laws. At its deepest point it is 406 ft.

The Starnbergersee is named after its chief resort, **STARNBERG**, the largest town on the lake and the nearest to Munich. Pleasure boats set off from the jetty for trips around the lake. The resort has a tree-lined lakeside promenade and some fine turn-of-the-20th-century villas, some of which are now hotels. There are abundant restaurants, taverns, and chestnut-tree-shaded beer gardens.

On the lake's eastern shore at the village of Berg you'll find the **KING LUDWIG II MEMORIAL CHAPEL.** A well-marked path leads through thick woods to the chapel, built near the point in the lake where the drowned king's body was found on June 13, 1886. He had been confined in nearby Berg Castle after the Bavarian government took action against his withdrawal from reality and his bankrupting castle-building fantasies. A cross in the lake marks the point where his body was recovered.

The castle of **POSSENHOFEN,** home of Ludwig's favorite cousin, Sisi, stands on the western shore, practically opposite Berg. Local lore says they used to send affectionate messages across the lake to each other. Sisi married the Austrian emperor Franz Joseph I but spent more than 20 summers in the lakeside castle, now a luxury hotel, the **Kaiserin Elisabeth.** *Tutzingerstr. 2–6, Feldafing, tel. 08157/93090, www.kaiserin-elisabeth.de.*

Just offshore is the tiny **ROSENINSEL** (Rose Island), where King Maximilian II built a summer villa. You can swim to its tree-fringed shores or sail across in a dinghy or on a Windsurfer (Possenhofen's boatyard is one of the lake's many rental points).

Where to Stay and Eat

$$$–$$$$ FORSTHAUS ILKA-HÖHE. This fine old country lodge is set amid meadows above the lake, an uphill stroll from the Tutzing station at the end of the S-6 suburban line. The walk is well worth the effort, for the Ilka-Höhe is one of the region's most attractive restaurants, with a view of the lake. Luncheons are priced in the middle range, dinners are far more exclusive. In summer dine on its vine-clad terrace. Reservations are essential, but dress is casual. *Auf der Ilkehöhe, Tutzing, tel. 08158/8242. Reservations essential. No credit cards. Closed Mon. and Tues., last 2 wks Dec., and weekends Jan.*

$$–$$$$ HOTEL SCHLOSS BERG. King Ludwig II spent his final days in the small castle of Berg, from which this comfortable hotel gets its name. It's on the edge of the castle park where Ludwig liked to walk and a stone's throw from where he drowned. The older, century-old main hotel building is on the lakeside, although a modern annex overlooks the lake from the woods. All rooms are spacious and elegantly furnished. The restaurant ($–$$$$) and waterside beer garden are favorite haunts of locals and weekenders. *Seestr. 17, D–82335 Berg, tel. 08151/9630, fax 08151/96352, www.hotelschlossberg.de. 50 rooms. Restaurant, sauna, bicycles, Internet, some pets allowed (fee), bar, beer garden; no a/c,. AE, MC, V.*

$–$$$ SEERESTAURANT UNDOSA. This restaurant is only a short walk from the Starnberg railroad station and boat pier. Most tables command a view of the lake, which provides some of the best fish specialties on the international menu. This is the place to try the mild-tasting *Renke*, a perch-type fish. *Seepromenade 1, tel. 08151/998–930. Reservations not accepted. AE, MC, V. Closed Mon., Tues. and most of Jan. and half of Feb.*

$$ FORSTHAUS AM SEE. The handsome, geranium-covered Forsthaus faces the lake, and so do most of the large, pine-wood furnished rooms. The excellent restaurant ($$$) has a daily-changing international menu, with lake fish a specialty. The hotel has its own lake access and boat pier, with a chestnut-shaded beer garden nearby. *Am See 1, D–82343 Possenhofen, tel. 08157/93010, fax 08157/4292. 20 rooms, 1 suite. Restaurant, Internet, beer garden, some pets allowed (fee). AE, MC, V.*

Starnbergersee A to Z

TRANSPORTATION TO AND FROM STARNBERGERSEE

Starnberg and the north end of the lake are a 25-minute drive from Munich on the A–95 Autobahn. Follow the signs to Garmisch and take the Starnberg exit. Country roads then skirt the west and east banks of the lake, but most are closed to the public.

The S-bahn 6 suburban line runs from Munich's central Marienplatz to Starnberg and three other towns on the lake's west bank: Possenhofen, Feldafing, and Tutzing. The journey from Marienplatz to Starnberg takes 35 minutes. The east bank of the lake can be reached by bus from the town of Wolfratshausen, the end of the S-bahn 7 suburban line.

VISITOR INFORMATION

The quickest way to visit the Starnbergersee area is by ship. On Saturday evenings, the good ship *Seeshaupt* has dancing and dinner.

➤**TOURIST INFORMATION:** *Seeshaupt* (tel. 08151/12023). **Tourismusverband Starnberger Fünf-Seen-Land** (Wittelsbacher Str. 2c, D–82319 Starnberg, tel. 08151/90600, fax 08151/906–090, www.starnberg.de).

AMMERSEE

40 km (25 mi) southwest of Munich.

The Ammersee, the "peasant lake," is the country cousin of the better-known, more cosmopolitan Starnbergersee (the prince lake), and, accordingly, many Bavarians (and tourists, too) like it all the more. Munich cosmopolites of centuries past thought it too distant for an excursion, not to mention too rustic. So the shores remained relatively free of villas and parks, and even though upscale holiday homes claim some stretches of the eastern shore, the Ammersee still offers more open areas for bathing and boating than the bigger lake to the west. Bicyclists circle the 19-km-long (12-mi-long) lake (it's nearly 6 km [4 mi] across at its widest point) on a path that rarely loses sight of the water. Hikers can spread out the tour for two or three days, staying overnight in any of the comfortable inns along the way. Dinghy sailors and windsurfers zip across in minutes with the help of the Alpine winds that swoop down from the mountains. A ferry cruises the lake at regular intervals during summer, stopping at several piers. Board it at Herrsching.

HERRSCHING has a delightful promenade, part of which winds through the resort's park. The 100-year-old villa that sits so comfortably there seems as if it were built by Ludwig II, such is the romantic and fanciful mixture of medieval turrets and Renaissance-style facades. It was actually built for the artist Ludwig Scheuermann in the late 19th century and became a favorite meeting place for Munich and Bavarian artists. It is now a municipal cultural center and the scene of chamber-music concerts on some summer weekends.

The Benedictine monastery of **ANDECHS,** one of southern Bavaria's most famous pilgrimage sites, lies 5 km (3 mi) south of Herrsching. You can reach it on Bus 951 (which also connects Ammersee and Starnbergersee). This extraordinary ensemble surmounted by an octagonal tower and onion dome with a pointed helmet has a busy history going back over 1,000 years. The church, originally built in the 15th century, was entirely redone in baroque style in the early 18th century. The **Heilige Kapelle** contains the remains of the old treasure of the Benedictines in Andechs, including Charlemagne's "Victory Cross," and a monstrance containing the three sacred hosts brought back from the crusades by the original rulers of the area, the Counts of Diessen-Andechs. One of the attached chapels contains the remains of composer Carl Orff. The church is being renovated completely in preparation for the 550th anniversary of the monastery in 2005. Crowds of pilgrims are drawn not only by the beauty of the hilltop monastery but by the beer brewed here (600,000 liters annually). The monastery makes its own cheese as well, and it's an excellent accompaniment to the rich, almost black beer. You can enjoy both at large wooden tables in the monastery tavern or on the terrace outside. *www.andechs.de.* Daily 7–7.

The little town of **DIESSEN** at the southwest corner of the lake has one of the most magnificent religious buildings of the whole region: the **Augustine abbey church of St. Mary.** No lesser figure than the great Munich architect Johann Michael Fischer designed this airy, early rococo edifice. François Cuvilié the Elder, whose work can be seen all over Munich, did the sumptuous gilt-and-marble high altar. Visit in late afternoon, when the light falls sharply on its crisp gray, white, and gold facade, etching the pencil-like tower and spire against the darkening sky over the lake. Don't leave without at least peeping into neighboring St. Stephen's courtyard, its cloisters smothered in wild roses. But Diessen is not all church. It has attracted artists and craftspeople since the early 20th century. Among the most famous who made his home here is the composer Carl Orff, author of numerous works inspired from medieval material, including the famous *Carmina Burana*, songs based on secular texts. His life and work—notably the pedagogical Schulwerk instruments—are exhibited in the **Carl-Orff-Museum** (Hofmark 3, tel. 08807/1583; weekends 2–5) and visitors are welcome to try them out.

Where to Stay and Eat

$$ AMMERSEE HOTEL. This very comfortable, modern resort hotel has views from an unrivaled position on the lakeside promenade. Rooms overlooking the lake are in big demand and more expensive. The Artis restaurant ($–$$) has an international menu. *Summerstr. 32, D–82211 Herrsching, tel. 08152/96870, fax 08152/5374. 40 rooms.*

Restaurant, cable TV, in-room data ports, gym, hot tub, sauna, some pets allowed (fee); no a/c. AE, DC, MC, V.

$$ LANDHOTEL PIUSHOF. In a parklike garden, the family-run Piushof has elegant Bavarian guest rooms, with lots of oak and hand-carved cupboards. The beamed and pillared restaurant ($$–$$$) has an excellent menu of Bavarian specialties, and the open fireplace radiates pure ambience. *Schönbichlstr. 18, D–82211 Herrsching, tel. 08152/96820, fax 08152/968–270, www.piushof.de. 21 rooms, 3 suites. Restaurant, cable TV, in-room data ports, tennis court, pool, massage, sauna, some pets allowed (fee); no a/c. MC, V.*

$ HOTEL GARNI ZUR POST. Families feel particularly at home here, and children amuse themselves at the playground and small deer park. Rooms are in Bavarian country style, with solid pine furnishings, and are clean and functional. A delicious breakfast buffet prepares guests for the long days a-visiting. *Starnberger Str. 2, D–82346 Andechs, tel. 08152/3433, fax 08152/2303. 32 rooms, 22 with bath. Cable TV, Internet, playground, some pets allowed (fee); no a/c. MC.*

$ HOTEL PROMENADE. From the hotel terrace restaurant ($–$$) you can watch the pleasure boats tie up at the pier. The menu satisfies smaller hungers with cheese and ham platters or warm snacks and Alpine appetites with traditional pork dishes (hocks [Schweinshaxe] or roast [Schweinsbraten]), to more delicate trout dishes (Forelle). If you're overnighting, ask for a lake room; they all have geranium-hung balconies. Those under the dormer-broken roof are particularly cozy. *Summerstr. 6, D–82211 Herrsching, tel. 08152/1088, fax 08152/5981. 11 rooms. Restaurant, café, cable TV, some pets allowed; no a/c. DC, MC, V. Closed Jan.*

Ammersee A to Z

TRANSPORTATION TO AND FROM AMMERSEE

Take Autobahn 96—follow the signs to Lindau—and 20 km (12 mi) west of Munich take the exit for Herrsching, the lake's principal town.

Herrsching is also the end of the S-bahn 5 suburban line, a 47-minute ride from Munich's Marienplatz. From the Herrsching train station, Bus 952 runs north along the lake, and Bus 951 runs south and continues on to Starnberg in a 40-minute journey.

Getting around on a boat is the best way to visit. Each town on the lake has a pier (*Anlegestelle*).

VISITOR INFORMATION

➤**TOURIST INFORMATION: Verkehrsbüro** (Bahnhofspl. 2, Herrsching, tel. 08152/5227; weekdays 8:30–noon).

DACHAU

20 km (12 mi) northwest of Munich.

Dachau predates Munich, with records going back to the time of Charlemagne. It's a handsome town, too, built on a hilltop with views of Munich and the Alps. A guided tour of the town, including the castle and church, leaves from the Rathaus on Saturday at 10:30, from May through mid-October. Dachau is better known worldwide as the site of the first Nazi concentration camp, which was built just outside it. Dachau preserves the memory of the camp and the horrors perpetrated there with deep contrition while trying, with commendable discretion, to signal that it also has other points of interest.

The site of the infamous camp, now the **KZ-GEDENKSTÄTTE DACHAU** (Dachau Concentration Camp Memorial), is just outside town. Photographs, contemporary documents, the few remaining cell blocks, and the grim crematorium (never used) create a somber and moving picture of the camp, where more than 30,000 of the 200,000-plus prisoners lost their lives. A documentary film in English is shown daily at 11:30 and 3:30. The former camp has become more than just a grisly memorial: it is now a place where people of all nations meet, to reflect upon the past and on the present. Several religious shrines and memorials have been built to honor the dead, who came from

Germany and all occupied nations. To reach the memorial by car, leave the center of the town along Schleissheimerstrasse and turn left into Alte Römerstrasse; the site is on the left. By public transport take Bus 724 or 726 from the Dachau S-bahn train station or the town center. Both stop within a two-minute walk from the site (ask the driver to let you out there). If you are driving from Munich, turn right on the first country road (marked B) before entering Dachau and follow the signs. *Alte Römerstr. 75, tel. 08131/996–880. Free. Tues.–Sun. 9–5. Guided English tour June–Aug., Tues.–Sun. 12:30; Sept.–May, weekends 12:30.*

SCHLOSS DACHAU, the hilltop castle, dominates the town. What you'll see is the one remaining wing of a palace built by the Munich architect Josef Effner for the Wittelsbach ruler Max Emanuel in 1715. During the Napoleonic Wars the palace served as a field hospital, treating French and Russian casualties from the Battle of Austerlitz (1805). The wars made a casualty, too, of the palace, and three of the four wings were demolished by order of King Max Joseph I. What's left is a handsome cream-and-white building, with an elegant pillared and lantern-hung café on the ground floor and a former ballroom above. About once a month the grand Renaissance hall, with a richly decorated and carved ceiling featuring painted panels depicting figures from ancient mythology, is used for chamber concerts. The east terrace affords panoramic views of Munich and, on fine days, the distant Alps. There's also a 250-year-old *Schlossbrauerei* (castle brewery), which hosts the town's beer and music festival each year in the first two weeks of August. *Schlosspl., tel. 08131/ 87923. €1; tour €2.50. May–Sept., weekends 2–5; tour of town and Schloss May–mid-Oct., Sat. 10:30.*

ST. JACOB, Dachau's parish church, was built in the early 16th century in late-Renaissance style on the foundations of a 14th-century Gothic structure. Baroque features and a characteristic onion dome were added in the late 17th century. On the south wall you can admire a very fine 17th-century sundial. A visit to the church is included in the guided tour of the town. *Konrad-Adenauer-Str. 7. Daily 7–7.*

An artists' colony formed here during the 19th century, and the tradition lives on. Picturesque houses line Hermann-Stockmann-Strasse and part of Münchner Strasse, and many of them are still the homes of successful artists. The **GEMÄLDEGALERIE** displays the works of many of the town's 19th-century artists. *Konrad-Adenauer-Str. 3, tel. 08131/567–516. €2. Wed.–Fri. 11–5, weekends 1–5.*

Where to Eat

$–$$ BRÄUSTÜBERL. Near the castle, the Bräustüberl has a shady beer garden for lunches and a cozy tavern for year-round Bavarian-style eating and drinking. *Schlossstr. 8, tel. 08131/72553. MC. Closed Mon.*

$–$$ WEILACHMÜHLE. You have to drive a ways for this absolute gem
★ of a restaurant–cum–beer garden–cum–stage and exhibition room in the little village of Thalhausen. It's in a farmhouse that was restored the way it should be, the old dark wooden door opening onto a generous dining area paneled in simple, light pine. The food is above reproach, beginning with the benchmark Schweinsbraten. To get to the Weilachmüle drive 26 km (16 mi) north toward Aichach, then take a right toward Thalhausen (2 km [1.25 mi]) in the village of Wollomoos. *Am Mühlberg 5, Thalhausen, tel. 08254/1711, www.weilachmuehle.de. No credit cards. Thurs.–Sat. 5 PM–midnight, Sun. 10:30 AM–11 PM; opens an hr later as of Oct. until mid- to end of Mar.*

$–$$ ZIEGLERBRÄU. Dachau's leading beer tavern, once a 17th-century brewer's home, is a warren of cozy, wood-paneled rooms where you'll probably share a table with a party of locals on a boys' night out. The food is solid varieties of pork, potato, and sausages in all forms. In summer the tables spill out onto the street for a very Italian feeling. If looking for a night out, the restaurant runs the neighboring nightclub. *Konrad-Adenauer-Str. 8, tel. 08131/4073. No credit cards.*

Dachau A to Z

TRANSPORTATION TO AND FROM DACHAU

Take the B–12 country road or the Stuttgart Autobahn to the Dachau exit from Munich. Dachau is also on the S-bahn 2 suburban line, a 20-minute ride from Munich's Marienplatz.

VISITOR INFORMATION

➤TOURIST INFORMATION: Verkehrsverein Dachau (Konrad-Adenauer-Str. 1, tel. 08131/75286, fax 08131/84529, www.dachau-info.de).

LANDSHUT

64 km (40 mi) north of Munich.

If fortune had placed Landshut south of Munich, in the protective folds of the Alpine foothills, instead of the same distance north, in the subdued flatlands of Lower Bavaria—of which it is the capital—the historic town would be teeming with tourists. Landshut's geographical misfortune is the discerning visitor's good luck, for the town is never overcrowded, with the possible exception of the three summer weeks when the *Landshuter Hochzeit* (Landshut Wedding) is celebrated. The next celebration is in 2005, and then a visit to Landshut is a must. The festival commemorates the marriage in 1475 of Prince George of Bavaria-Landshut, son of the expressively named Ludwig the Rich, to Princess Hedwig, daughter of the king of Poland. Within its ancient walls, the entire town is swept away in a colorful reconstruction of the event. The wedding procession, with the "bride" and "groom" on horseback, accompanied by pipes and drums and the hurly-burly of a medieval pageant, is held on three consecutive weekends, while a medieval-style fair fills the central streets throughout the three weeks.

Landshut has two magnificent cobblestone market streets. The one in **ALTSTADT** (Old Town) is one of the most beautiful city streets in Germany; the other is in **Neustadt** (New Town). The two streets run parallel to each other, tracing a course between the Isar River and the heights overlooking the town. A steep path from Altstadt takes you up to **BURG TRAUSNITZ**. This castle was begun in 1204 and accommodated the Wittelsbach dukes of Bavaria-Landshut until 1503. *Tel. 0871/22638. €2.50 including guided tour. Apr.–Sept., daily 9–noon and 1–5; Oct.–Mar., Tues.–Sun. 10–noon and 1–4.*

The **STADTRESIDENZ** in Altstadt was the first Italian Renaissance building of its kind north of the Alps. It was built from 1536 to 1537, but was given a baroque facade at the end of the 19th century. The Wittelsbachs lived here during the 16th century. The facade of the palace forms an almost modest part of the architectural splendor and integrity of the Altstadt, where even the ubiquitous McDonald's has to serve its hamburgers behind a baroque exterior. The Residenz includes exhibitions on the history of Landshut. *Altstadt 79, Altstadt, tel. 0871/22638. €2. Apr.–Sept., daily 9–noon and 1–5; Oct.–Mar., 10–noon and 1–4.*

The **RATHAUS** (Town Hall) stands opposite the Stadtresidenz, an elegant, light-colored building with a typical neo-Gothic roof design. It was originally a set of 13th-century burgher houses, taken over by the town in the late 1300s. The famous bride and groom allegedly danced in the grand ceremonial hall, with its heavy wood paneling and rows of frescoes, during their much celebrated wedding in 1475. The tourist information is on the ground floor. *Altstadt 315, tel. 0871/922–050. Free. Mon.–Fri. 2–3, and on official tours.*

The **MARTINSKIRCHE** (St. Martin's), with the tallest brick church tower (436 ft) in the world, soars above the other buildings with its bristling spire. The church contains some magnificent Gothic treasures and a 16th-century carved Madonna. It is surely the only church in the world to contain an image of Hitler, albeit in a devilish pose. The führer and other Nazi leaders are portrayed as executioners in a 1946 stained-glass window showing the martyrdom of St. Kastulus. In the nave of the church is a clear and helpful description of its history and treasures in English. *Corner of Altstadt and Kirchg, tel. 0871/24277. Apr.–Sept., daily 7–6:30; Oct.– Mar., daily 7–5.*

Built into a steep slope of the hill crowned by Burg Trausnitz is an unusual art museum, the **SKULPTURENMUSEUM IM HOFBERG**, containing the entire collection of the Landshut sculptor Fritz Koenig. His own work forms the permanent central section of the labyrinthine gallery. *Kolpingstr. 481, tel. 0871/89021. €3. Tues.–Sun. 10:30–1 and 2–5.*

OFF THE **FREISING** – Freising (at the end of the S-bahn 1 line, a 45-minute
BEATEN ride from central Munich) is an ancient episcopal seat and its
PATH cathedral and Old Town are well worth including in a visit to
Landshut, 35 km (22 mi) to the northeast.

Where to Stay and Eat

There are several attractive Bavarian-style restaurants in the Altstadt and Neustadt, most of them with beer gardens. Although Landshut brews a fine beer, look for a *Gaststätte* offering a *Weihenstephaner*, from the world's oldest brewery, in Freising. Helles (light) is the most popular beer variety.

$$-$$$ **LINDNER HOTEL KAISERHOF.** The green Isar River rolls outside the bedroom windows of Landshut's most distinctive hotel. Its steep red roof and white facade blend harmoniously with the waterside panorama. The "Herzog Ludwig" restaurant ($$) serves a sumptuous but reasonably priced lunch buffet and is an elegant place for dinner. *Papiererstr. 2, D–84034, tel. 0871/6870, fax 0871/ 687–403, www.lindner.de. 144 rooms. Restaurant, cable TV with movies and video games, in-room data ports, gym, sauna, steam room, meeting rooms, bicycles, pets allowed (fee); no a/c in some rooms, no-smoking rooms. AE, DC, MC, V.*

$$ HOTEL GOLDENE SONNE. The steeply gabled Renaissance facade of the Golden Sun fronts a hotel of great charm and sleek comfort. It stands in the center of town, near all the sights. Its dining options are a paneled, beamed restaurant ($$–$$$), a vaulted cellar, and a courtyard beer garden, where the service is smilingly, helpfully Bavarian. The menu follows the seasons and toes the "quintessential Bavarian" line, with much pork roast, trout steamed or smoked with horseradish, asparagus in the spring (usually accompanied by potatoes or ham), venison in the fall. *Neustadt 520, D–84028, tel. 0871/92530, fax 0871/925–3350, www.goldenesonne.de. 55 rooms. Restaurant, beer garden, pub, cable TV, in-room data ports, some pets allowed (fee); no a/c, no-smoking rooms. AE, DC, MC, V.*

$$ ROMANTIK HOTEL FÜRSTENHOF. This handsome Landshut city mansion had no difficulty qualifying for inclusion in the Romantik group of hotels—it just breathes romance, from its plush little restaurant ($$$) all covered in wood paneling, to the cozy bedrooms. A vine-covered terrace shadowed by a chestnut tree adds charm. *Stethaimerstr. 3, D–84034, tel. 0871/92550, fax 0871/925–544, www.romantikhotels.com/landshut. 24 rooms. Restaurant, cable TV, Internet, sauna; no a/c in some rooms, no-smoking rooms. AE, DC, MC, V. Restaurant closed Sun.*

$$ SCHLOSS SCHÖNBRUNN. This country mansion is now a luxurious hotel, with many of the original features intact. Rooms in the most historic part of the building are particularly attractive, with huge double beds, and represent excellent value. The handsome house stands in the Schönbrunn district of Landshut, about 2 km (1 mi) from the center. The journey is worthwhile even for the excellent restaurant ($$–$$$), where the menu includes fish from the hotel's own pond. *Schönbrunn 1, D–84036, tel. 0871/95220, fax 0871/952–2222, www.hotel-schoenbrunn.de. 33 rooms. Restaurant, café, cable TV, in-room data ports, bar, beer garden, some pets allowed (fee); no a/c, no-smoking rooms. AE, DC, MC, V.*

Landshut A to Z

TRANSPORTATION TO AND FROM LANDSHUT

Landshut is a 45-minute drive northwest from Munich on either the A–92 Autobahn—follow the signs to Deggendorf—or the B–11 highway. The Plattling–Regensburg–Passau train line brings you from Munich in about 50 minutes. A round trip costs about €20.

VISITOR INFORMATION

➤TOURIST INFORMATION: Verkehrsverein (Altstadt 315, tel. 0871/922–050, www.landshut.de). Landshut Wedding 2005 celebration (tel. 0871/22918, fax 0871/274–653).

WASSERBURG AM INN

51 km (30 mi) east of Munich.

Wasserburg floats like a faded ship of state in a lazy loop of the Inn River, which comes within a few yards of cutting the ancient town off from the wooded slopes of the encroaching countryside. Wasserburg was once an important trading post, owing in great part to the still extant Red Bridge (Rote Brücke). Later it was luckily ignored by the industrialization that gripped Germany in the 19th century. You're never more than 100 yards or so from the river in the **ALTSTADT**, which huddles within the walls of the castle that originally gave the town its name. The almost Italian look is typical of many Inn River towns. Use the north- or east-bank parking lot as the town is expanding the traffic-free zone. It's only a few minutes' walk to the central Marienplatz. There you'll find Wasserburg's late-Gothic brick **Rathaus.** The Bavarian regional government met here until 1804, deliberating in its beautifully decorated Renaissance *Ratsstube* (council chamber). Opposite the Rathaus is the baroque facade of the Kern house, designed by architect Johann Baptist Zimmermann from Munich. He actually merely pasted two houses together, as it were, and added a glorious front in 1738. *Marienpl. €.75. Guided tour Tues.–Fri. at 10, 11, 2, 3, and 4; weekends at 10 and 11.*

The 14th-century **FRAUENKIRCHE** (Church of Our Lady), on Marienplatz, is the town's oldest church. The 213-ft tower was once a city watchtower, and the church was given its baroque style in 1753. The baroque altar frames a Madonna sitting on a throne with a view of Wasserburg in the background. Wasserburg's imposing 15th-century parish church, **ST. JAKOB** (Kirchhofpl.), has an intricately carved baroque pulpit dating from 1640.

Next to the 14th-century town gate, at the end of Wasserburg's Rote Brücke, is the **ERSTES IMAGINÄRES MUSEUM** (First Imaginary Museum). The museum, which is housed in the former Holy Ghost Hospital, has a collection of more than 500 world-famous paintings, but without an original among them; every single one is a precise copy, executed by various artists. This was the idea of the late Günter Dietz, an artist and stage painter, who felt those who couldn't travel the world to see the originals could still appreciate the far-flung masterpieces here. €1.50. May–Sept., Tues.–Sun. 11–5; Oct.–Apr., Tues.–Sun. 1–5.

Wasserburg is a convenient base for walks along the banks of the Inn River and into the countryside. A pretty path west leads to the village of **ATTEL**. Another half hour into the Attel River valley, and you'll reach the enchanting castle-restaurant of **Schloss Hart** (tel. 08039/1774).

Where to Stay and Eat

$–$$ HOTEL FLETZINGER BRÄU. Wasserburg's leading hotel began as a brewery, and you can sample local ales in its noisy, friendly tavern. Rooms are large and homey; many have original antiques. *Fletzingerg. 1, D–83512, tel. 08071/90890, fax 08071/909–8177, hotel-fletzinger.com. 40 rooms. Restaurant, cable TV, in-room data ports, beer garden, pub, some pets allowed (fee). AE, MC, V.*

$ HERRENHAUS. This is one of Wasserburg's oldest houses, with medieval foundations and a centuries-old wine cellar. Pork dishes with dumplings and sauerkraut are served at the oak tables beneath vaulted ceilings. In summer the beer garden opens at 4 PM. *Herreng. 17, tel. 08071/2800. MC. Closed Mon. No dinner Sun.*

$ PAULANERSTUBEN. If you want to know what living in the glorious Kern Haus is like, try one of the rooms of the remarkable good-value Paulanerstuben. The quieter rear rooms look out onto the river or onto the courtyard. Solid Bavarian cooking welcomes you, with a strong nod to Mediterranean dishes for the vegetarians (ratatouille stuffed pancakes, for example). You will share space with other Wasserburgians. *Marienpl. 9, tel. 08071/3903, fax 08071/50474, paulanerstuben-wasserburg.de. Restaurant, cable TV, some pets allowed; no a/c. No credit cards. Closed Jan.*

Wasserburg A to Z

TRANSPORTATION TO AND FROM WASSERBURG
Take the B–304 from Munich, which leads directly to Wasserburg. It's a 45-minute drive. The S-bahn 4 suburban line goes to Ebersberg, where you'll have to change to a local train to Wasserburg, or the Salzburg express, changing at Grafing Bahnhof to the local line. Both trips take 90 minutes.

VISITOR INFORMATION
➤**TOURIST INFORMATION: Verkehrsamt** (Rathauspl. 1, D–83512 Wasserburg am Inn, tel. 08071/10522, www.wasserburg.de; weekdays 9–3, Sat. 10–1).

practical information

Addresses

In this book the words for street (*Strasse*) and alley (*Gasse*) are abbreviated as str. and g. within italicized service information. Brüdergasse will appear as Brüderg., for example.

Airports

Some airlines have nonstop flights to Munich's International Airport from North America. The very modern airport is 28 km (17 mi) northeast of the city center, between the small towns of Freising and Erding. In mid-2003, the new Terminal 2 will open as the exclusive terminal for Star Alliance members, which includes Lufthansa, Air Canada, and United, among other airlines.

➤AIRPORT INFORMATION: Fluhafen München (tel. 089/ 97500, www.munich-airport.de).

AIRPORT TRANSFERS

A fast train service links the airport with Munich's main train station. The S-1 and S-8 lines operate from a terminal directly beneath the airport's arrival and departure halls. Trains leave every 10 minutes, and the journey takes around 40 minutes. Stops along the way include the Ostbahnhof (convenient for lodgings east of the Isar River) and such city-center stations as Marienplatz. A one-way ticket costs €8, or €7.20 if you purchase a multiple-use "strip" ticket (you will have two strips left at the end). A family of up to five (two adults and three children under 15) can make the trip for €15 by buying a Tageskarte ticket (which allows travel until around 6 AM the next morning). The bus service is slower than the S-bahn link (€9 one-way, €14.50 round-trip). A taxi from the airport costs around €50. During rush hours (7 AM–10 AM and 4 PM–7 PM), allow up to an hour of traveling time. If you're driving from the airport to the city, take route A–9 and follow the signs for MÜNCHEN STADTMITTE. If you're driving from the city center, head north through Schwabing, join the A–9 Autobahn at the Frankfurter Ring intersection, and follow the signs for the airport (FLUGHAFEN).

Bike Travel

The city is threaded with a network of bike paths, and bikes are allowed on the S-bahn (except from 6 AM to 9 AM and from 4 PM to 6 PM). Bicycles on public transportation cost either one strip on a multiple ticket, or € 2.50 for a day ticket, € 0.90 for a single ticket. A free map showing all bike trails is available at all city tourist offices.

Bikes can be rented from April through October at the Hauptbahnhof and at some S-bahn and mainline stations around Munich. A list of stations that offer the service is available from the Deutsche Bahn. The cost is €3.80–€12.50 a day depending on the type of bike.

➤BIKE RENTALS: Aktiv-Rad (Hans-Sachs-Str. 7, Isarvorstadt, tel. 089/266–506). the bike and walk company GmbH (Tal 31, City Center, tel. 089/5895–8930). Hauptbahnhof (Radius Touristik, opposite platform 31, Leopoldvorstadt, tel. 089/596–113). Will Fahrradverleih (Kleinhesselohe 4 [at the Kleinhesselohe Lake in the Englischer Garten], Schwabing, tel. 089/338–353).

Bus Travel to and from Munich

Long-distance buses arrive and depart from an area to the west of the main train station. The actual office of the bus company, Touring GmbH, is in the northern section of the train station itself, an area referred to as the Starnberger Bahnhof.

►**BUS STATION: Zentraler Busbahnhof** (Arnulfstr., Leopold-vorstadt, tel. 089/545–8700).

Car Rental

Rates with the major car-rental companies begin at about €75 per day and €300 per week, including value-added tax, for an economy car with a manual transmission and unlimited mileage. Volkswagen, Opel, and Mercedes are some standard brands of rentals; most rentals are manual, so if you want an automatic, be sure to **request one in advance**. If you're traveling with children, don't forget to **arrange for a car seat** when you reserve.

All Hauptbahnhof (train station) offices are in the mezzanine-level gallery above the Deutsche Bahn information and ticket center. Airport offices are in the central area, Zentralbereich.

►**LOCAL AGENCIES: Avis** (Airport, tel. 089/9759–7600; Hauptbahnhof, Leopoldvorstadt, tel. 089/550–2251). **Europcar** (Airport, tel. 089/973–5020; Hauptbahnhof, Leopoldvorstadt, tel. 089/549–0240, www.europcar.de). **Hertz** (Airport, tel. 089/978–860; Hauptbahnhof, Leopoldvorstadt, tel. 089/550–2256). **Sixt** (Airport, tel. 089/526–2525; Hauptbahnhof, Leopoldvorstadt, tel. 089/550–2447).

Car Travel

From the north (Nürnberg or Frankfurt), leave the autobahn at the Schwabing exit. From Stuttgart and the west, the autobahn ends at Obermenzing, Munich's most westerly suburb. The autobahns from Salzburg and the east, Garmisch and the south, and Lindau and the southwest all join the Mittlerer Ring (city beltway). When leaving any autobahn, follow the signs reading STADTMITTE for downtown Munich.

RULES OF THE ROAD

There are posted speed limits on autobahns, and drivers are advised to keep below 130 kph (80 mph). Alcohol limits on drivers are equivalent to two small beers or a quarter of a liter of wine (blood-alcohol level .05%). Note that **seat belts must be worn at all times by front- *and* backseat passengers.** Passing is permitted on the left side only. Headlights, not parking lights, are required during inclement weather. Don't enter streets with signposts bearing a red circle with a white horizontal stripe— they are one-way streets. The blue sign EINBAHNSTRASSE (one-way) indicates you have the right of way. A right turn on a red light is permitted only if there is also a green arrow.

PARKING

Parking in Munich is nervewracking and not cheap. There are several parking garages throughout the center, but your best bet is to use public transportation, which is exemplary.

Consulates

➤**CANADA: Canadian Consulate** (Tal 29, City Center, tel. 089/ 219–9570).

➤**UNITED KINGDOM: British Consulate General** (Bürkleinstr. 10, Lehel, tel. 089/211–090).

➤**UNITED STATES: U.S. Consulate General** (Königinstr. 5, Maxvorstadt, tel. 089/28880).

Customs and Duties

When shopping abroad, **keep receipts** for all purchases. Upon reentering the country, **be ready to show customs officials what**

you've bought. If you feel a duty is incorrect, appeal the assessment. If you object to the way your clearance was handled, note the inspector's badge number. In either case, first ask to see a supervisor. If the problem isn't resolved, write to the appropriate authorities, beginning with the port director at your point of entry.

IN AUSTRALIA

Australian residents who are 18 or older may bring home A$400 worth of souvenirs and gifts (including jewelry), 250 cigarettes or 250 grams of tobacco, and 1,125 ml of alcohol (including wine, beer, and spirits). Residents under 18 may bring back A$200 worth of goods. Prohibited items include meat products. Seeds, plants, and fruits need to be declared upon arrival.

➤INFORMATION: **Australian Customs Service** (Regional Director, Box 8, Sydney, NSW 2001, tel. 02/9213–2000 or 1300/363263, fax 02/9213–4000, www.customs.gov.au).

IN CANADA

Canadian residents who have been out of Canada for at least seven days may bring in C$750 worth of goods duty-free. If you've been away fewer than seven days but more than 48 hours, the duty-free allowance drops to C$200; if your trip lasts 24 to 48 hours, the allowance is C$50. You may not pool allowances with family members. Goods claimed under the C$750 exemption may follow you by mail; those claimed under the lesser exemptions must accompany you. Alcohol and tobacco products may be included in the seven-day and 48-hour exemptions but not in the 24-hour exemption. If you meet the age requirements of the province or territory through which you reenter Canada, you may bring in, duty-free, 1.5 liters of wine or 1.14 liters (40 imperial ounces) of liquor or 24 12-ounce cans or bottles of beer or ale. If you are 19 or older you may bring in, duty-free, 200 cigarettes and 50 cigars. Check ahead of time with the Canada Customs and Revenue Agency or the Department of Agriculture for policies regarding meat products, seeds, plants, and fruits.

You may send an unlimited number of gifts (only one gift per recipient, however) worth up to C$60 each duty-free to Canada. Label the package UNSOLICITED GIFT—VALUE UNDER $60. Alcohol and tobacco are excluded.

➤**INFORMATION: Canada Customs and Revenue Agency** (2265 St. Laurent Blvd. S, Ottawa, Ontario K1G 4K3, tel. 204/ 983–3500; 506/636–5064; 800/461–9999 in Canada, www. ccra-adrc.gc.ca/).

IN GERMANY

Since a single, unrestricted market took effect within the European Union (EU) early in 1993, there have no longer been restrictions for persons traveling among the 15 EU countries. However, there are restrictions on what can be brought in without declaration. For example, if you have more than 800 cigarettes, 90 liters of wine, or 10 liters of alcohol, it is considered a commercial shipment and is taxed and otherwise treated as such.

For anyone entering Germany from outside the EU, the following limitations apply: (1) 200 cigarettes or 100 cigarillos or 50 cigars or 250 grams of tobacco; (2) 2 liters of still table wine; (3) 1 liter of spirits over 22% volume or 2 liters of spirits under 22% volume (fortified and sparkling wines) or 2 more liters of table wine; (4) 50 grams of perfume and 250 milliliters of toilet water; (5) 500 grams of roasted coffee or 200 grams of instant coffee; (6) other goods to the value of €175.

Tobacco and alcohol allowances are for visitors age 17 and over. Other items intended for personal use can be imported and exported freely. If you bring in cash, checks, securities, precious metals, or jewelry with a value of more than €15,000, you must tell the customs people where you got it and what you intend to do with it. This is a new measure for fighting money laundering.

If you have questions regarding customs or bringing a pet into the country, contact the Zoll-Infocenter, preferably by mail or e-mail.

➤**INFORMATION: Zoll-Infocenter** (Hansaallee 141, D–60320 Frankfurt am Main, tel. 069/469976-00, fax 069/469976–99).

IN NEW ZEALAND

All homeward-bound residents may bring back NZ$700 worth of souvenirs and gifts; passengers may not pool their allowances, and children can claim only the concession on goods intended for their own use. For those 17 or older, the duty-free allowance also includes 4.5 liters of wine or beer; one 1,125-ml bottle of spirits; and either 200 cigarettes, 250 grams of tobacco, 50 cigars, or a combination of the three up to 250 grams. Meat products, seeds, plants, and fruits must be declared upon arrival to the Agricultural Services Department.

➤**INFORMATION: New Zealand Customs** (Head Office, The Customhouse, 17–21 Whitmore St., Box 2218, Wellington, tel. 09/300–5399 or 0800/428–786, www.customs.govt.nz).

IN THE U.K.

If you are a U.K. resident and your journey was wholly within the European Union, you probably won't have to pass through customs when you return to the United Kingdom. If you plan to bring back large quantities of alcohol or tobacco, check EU limits beforehand. In most cases, if you bring back more than 200 cigars, 800 cigarettes, 10 liters of spirits, and/or 90 liters of wine, you have to declare the goods upon return.

➤**INFORMATION: HM Customs and Excise** (Portcullis House, 21 Cowbridge Rd. E, Cardiff CF11 9SS, tel. 029/2038–6423 or 0845/010–9000, www.hmce.gov.uk).

IN THE U.S.

U.S. residents who have been out of the country for at least 48 hours may bring home, for personal use, $400 worth of foreign goods duty-free, as long as they haven't used the $400 allowance or any part of it in the past 30 days. This exemption may include 1 liter of alcohol (for travelers 21 and older), 200 cigarettes, and 100 non-Cuban cigars. Family members from the same household who are traveling together may pool their $400 personal exemptions. For fewer than 48 hours, the duty-free allowance drops to $200, which may include 50 cigarettes, 10 non-Cuban cigars, and 150 milliliters of alcohol (or perfume containing alcohol). The $200 allowance cannot be combined with other individuals' exemptions, and if you exceed it, the full value of all the goods will be taxed. Antiques, which the U.S. Customs Service defines as objects more than 100 years old, enter duty-free, as do original works of art done entirely by hand, including paintings, drawings, and sculptures.

You may also send packages home duty-free, with a limit of one parcel per addressee per day (except alcohol or tobacco products or perfume worth more than $5). You can mail up to $200 worth of goods for personal use; label the package PERSONAL USE and attach a list of its contents and their retail value. If the package contains your used personal belongings, mark it PERSONAL GOODS RETURNED to avoid paying duties. You may send up to $100 worth of goods as a gift; mark the package UNSOLICITED GIFT. Mailed items do not affect your duty-free allowance on your return.

➤INFORMATION: **U.S. Customs Service** (for inquiries, 1300 Pennsylvania Ave. NW, Washington, DC 20229, www.customs. gov, tel. 202/354–1000; for complaints, Customer Satisfaction Unit, 1300 Pennsylvania Ave. NW, Room 5.5A, Washington, DC 20229; for registration of equipment, Office of Passenger Programs, 1300 Pennsylvania Ave. NW, Room 5.4D, Washington, DC 20229, tel. 202/927–0530).

Dining

Almost every street of Germany has its *Gaststätte*, a sort of combination diner and pub serving good home cooking at reasonable prices. A *Bierstube* (pub) or *Weinstube* (wine cellar) may also serve light snacks or meals. Service can be slow, but you'll also never experience being rushed out of your seat. Something else that may seem jarring at first: people can, and do, join other parties at a table in a restaurant if seating is tight. It is common courtesy to ask first, though.

MEALS AND SPECIALTIES

Most hotels serve a buffet-style breakfast (Frühstück) of rolls, cheese, cold cuts, eggs, cereals, yogurt, and spreads, which is often included in the price of a room. Cafés offer a similar choice, accompanied by coffee, tea, or Milchkaffee—a milky coffee that is rarely available at other times of the day.

Lunch (Mittagessen) is generally light. You can get sandwiches from most cafés and from bakeries, and many restaurants have special lunch menus that are often cheaper than in the evenings.

Dinner (Abendessen) is usually an à la carte affair. A substantial salad often comes with the main dish.

MEALTIMES

Gaststätte normally serve hot meals from 11:30 AM to 9 PM; many places stop serving hot meals between 2 PM and 6 PM, although you can still order cold dishes. Unless otherwise noted, the restaurants listed in this guide are open daily for lunch and dinner.

Electricity

To use electric-powered equipment purchased in the United States or Canada, **bring a converter and adapter.** The electrical current in Germany is 220 volts, 50 cycles alternating current (AC); wall outlets take Continental-type plugs, with two round prongs. If your appliances are dual-voltage, you'll need only an adapter. Don't use 110-volt outlets marked FOR SHAVERS ONLY for high-wattage appliances such as blow-dryers. Most laptops operate equally well on 110 and 220 volts and so require only an adapter.

Emergencies

Police (tel. 110). **Fire department, ambulance, and medical emergencies** (tel. 112).

English-Language Media

The monthly English-language magazine *Munich Found* is sold at most newspaper stands and in many hotels. It contains excellent listings, reviews restaurants and shows, and generally gives an idea of life in the city.

The Anglia English Bookshop is the leading English-language bookstore in Munich, although the shop is in incredible disorder, the books are very expensive (even the damaged ones), and the owner tends to make customers feel like intruders. But having overcome the mess, the suspicious looks, and the price, you'll find the selection is unimpeachable. Hugendubel has a good selection geared more toward novels and such. The Internationale Presse store is at the main train station. Words'worth is a well-kept shop with books in English.

Plays, readings, and other events are held in English at the Amerikahaus and at the British Council; both maintain reading rooms with a wealth of books and magazines. Amerikahaus's reading room is sunny and open from 1 to 5. If you're just looking for some light literature or inexpensive German-language coffee-table books, try text; the English language section is in the basement.

➤BOOKSTORES: **Anglia English Bookshop** (Schellingstr. 3, Schwabing, tel. 089/283–642). **Hugendubel** (Marienpl. 22, 2nd floor, City Center, tel. 089/23890 or 01803/484–484; Karlspl. 3, City Center, tel. 089/552–2530). **Internationale Presse** (tel. 089/13080). **texxt** (Sendlinger-Str. 24, City Center, tel. 089/2694–9503). **Words'worth** (Schellingstr. 21a, Schwabing, tel. 089/280–9141).

➤**ENGLISH-LANGUAGE EVENTS: Amerikahaus** (Karolinenpl. 3, near Königspl., Maxvorstadt, tel. 089/552–5370). **British Council** (Rumfordstr. 7, near Isartor, Isarvorstadt, tel. 089/ 290–0860).

Etiquette and Behavior

In restaurants, shops, and department stores, you are unlikely to be offered help unless you ask for it. The presumption is that you would prefer to be alone unless you indicate otherwise. Being on time for appointments, even casual social ones, is very important. Germans are more formal in addressing each other than Americans. Always address acquaintances as Herr (Mr.) or Frau (Mrs.) plus their last name; do not call them by their first name unless invited to do so. The German language has an informal and formal pronoun for "you": formal is "Sie," informal is "du." Even if adults are on a first-name basis with one another, they may still keep the Sie form between them. A handshake is expected upon meeting someone for the first time and is often customary when simply greeting acquaintances. Germans are less formal when it comes to nudity: a sign that reads FREIKÖRPER or FKK indicates a park or beach allows nude sunbathing.

Holidays

The following national holidays are observed in Munich: January 1; January 6 (Epiphany); April 18 (Good Friday); April 21 (Easter Monday); May 1 (Workers' Day); May 29 (Ascension); June 9 (Pentecost Monday); June 19 (Corpus Christi); August 15 (Assumption Day); October 3 (German Unity Day); November 1 (All Saints' Day); December 24–26 (Christmas).

Lodging

The standards of German hotels are very high, down to the humblest inn. You can nearly always **expect courteous and polite service and clean and comfortable rooms.** Most hotels have restaurants, but those listed as *Garni* provide breakfast only. The hotels in our listings are divided by price into four categories: $$$$, $$$, $$, and $. The lodgings we list are the cream of the crop in each price category. Properties are assigned price categories based on the range from their least-expensive standard double room at high season (excluding holidays) to the most expensive. We always list the facilities that are available—but we don't specify whether they cost extra. **Ask about breakfast and bathing facilities** when booking. A Continental breakfast is often included in the rate. All hotels listed have a private bath or shower unless otherwise noted.

HOTELS

Most hotels in Germany do not have air-conditioning, nor do they need it given the climate and the German style of building construction that uses thick walls and recessed windows to help keep the heat out. Smaller hotels do not provide much in terms of bathroom amenities. You may have to request a washcloth. Hotels often have no-smoking rooms or even no-smoking floors, so it's always worth asking for one when you reserve. Note that the beds in double rooms often consist of two twin mattresses placed side by side within a frame. When you arrive, if you don't like the room you're offered, ask to see another.

Mail and Shipping

Post offices (*Deutsche Post*) are recognizable by the postal symbol, a black bugle on a yellow background. Stamps (*Briefmarken*) can also be bought at some news agencies and souvenir shops. Post offices are generally open weekdays 8–6, Saturday 8–1. Airmail letters to the United States, Canada, Australia, and New Zealand cost €1.53; postcards, €1.02. All letters to the United Kingdom cost €.66; postcards, €.51.

Money Matters

ATMS

Twenty-four-hour ATMs (*Geldautomaten*) can be accessed with PLUS or Cirrus credit and banking cards. Some German banks exact €2–€5 fees for use of their ATMs. Your PIN number should be set for four digits; if it's longer, change it at your bank before the trip. Since some ATM keypads show no letters, **know the numeric equivalent of your password.**

CREDIT CARDS

All major U.S. credit cards are accepted in Germany. If you have a four-digit PIN number for your card, you can use it at German ATMs.

Throughout this guide, the following abbreviations are used: **AE,** American Express; **DC,** Diners Club; **MC,** MasterCard; and **V,** Visa.

➤**REPORTING LOST CARDS: American Express** (tel. 01805/840–840). **Diners Club** (tel. 05921/861–234). **MasterCard** (tel. 0800/819–1040). **Visa** (tel. 08008/149–100).

CURRENCY

Germany shares a common currency, the euro (€), with 11 other countries: Austria, Belgium, Finland, France, Greece, Ireland, Italy, Luxembourg, Netherlands, Portugal, and Spain. The euro is divided into 100 cents. There are bills of 5, 10, 20, 50, 100, and 500 euros and coins of €1 and €2, and 1, 2, 5, 10, 20, and 50 cents. For the most favorable currency exchange rates, **change money through banks.** Although ATM transaction fees may be higher abroad than at home, ATM rates are excellent because they are based on wholesale rates offered only by major banks. You won't do as well at exchange booths in airports or rail and bus stations, in hotels, in restaurants, or in stores.

Passports and Visas

When traveling internationally, **carry your passport** even if you don't need one (it's always the best form of I.D.) and **make two photocopies of the data page** (one for someone at home and another for you, carried separately from your passport). If you lose your passport, promptly call the nearest embassy or consulate and the local police.

ENTERING GERMANY

U.S., Canadian, Australian, New Zealand, and British citizens need only a valid passport to enter Germany for stays of up to 90 days.

Pharmacies

Internationale Ludwigs-Apotheke and Europa-Apotheke, both open weekdays 8–6 and Saturday 8–1, stock a large variety of over-the-counter medications. Munich pharmacies stay open late on a rotating basis, and every pharmacy has a schedule in its window.

➤**CONTACTS: Internationale Ludwigs-Apotheke** (Neuhauserstr. 11, City Center, tel. 089/260–3021). **Europa-Apotheke** (Schützenstr. 12, near the Hauptbahnhof, Leopoldvorstadt, tel. 089/595–423).

Taxes

VALUE-ADDED TAX

Most prices you see on items already have Germany's 16% value-added tax (VAT) included. When traveling to a non-EU country, you are entitled to a refund of the VAT you pay (multiply the price of an item by .138 to find out how much VAT is embedded in the price). Some goods, such as books and antiquities, carry a 7% VAT as a percentage of the purchase price. An item must cost at least €25 to qualify for a VAT refund.

When making a purchase, **ask for a V.A.T. refund form** and find out whether the merchant gives refunds—not all stores do, nor are they required to. Have the form stamped like any customs form by customs officials when you leave the country or, if you're visiting several European Union countries, when you leave the EU. Be ready to show customs officials what you've bought (pack purchases together, in your carry-on luggage); budget extra time for this. Take the form to a refund-service counter for an on-the-spot refund, or mail it back to the store or a refund service after you arrive home.

A refund service can save you some hassle, for a fee. Global Refund is a Europe-wide service with 130,000 affiliated stores and more than 700 refund counters—located at every major airport and border crossing. Its refund form is called a Shopping Cheque. The service issues refunds in the form of cash, check, or credit-card adjustment, minus a processing fee. If you don't have time to wait at the refund counter, you can mail in the form instead.

When departing from Munich for home, you can claim your VAT refund for purchases at a counter near the customs office, either between areas A and B, or between B and C. In mid-2003, Terminal 2 will also have a refund counter in the departure area between check-in and security.

➤**V.A.T. REFUNDS: Global Refund** (99 Main St., Suite 307, Nyack, NY 10960, tel. 800/566–9828, fax 845/348–1549, www.globalrefund.com). **Munich Airport Vat Refund Office** (tel. 089/975–92960).

Taxis

Munich's cream-color taxis are numerous. Hail them in the street or phone for one (there's an extra charge of €1 if you call). Rates start at €2.40. Expect to pay €8–€10 for a short trip within the city. There is a €0.50 charge for each piece of luggage.

➤**TAXI COMPANIES:** tel. 089/21610 or 089/19410.

Telephones

AREA AND COUNTRY CODES

The country code for Germany is 49. When dialing a German number from abroad, drop the initial "0" from the local area code. The country code is 001 for the United States and Canada, 0061 for Australia, 0064 for New Zealand, 0044 for the United Kingdom, 00353 for Ireland, and 0027 for South Africa.

DIRECTORY AND OPERATOR ASSISTANCE

If you have difficulty reaching your number, call 0180/200–1033. You can book collect calls through this number to the United States but not to other countries. For information in English dial 11837 for numbers within Germany, and 11834 for numbers elsewhere. But first **look for the number in the phone book or on the Web** (www.teleauskunft.de), because directory assistance is costly. Calls to 11837 and 11834 cost at least €.50, more if the call lasts more than 30 seconds.

INTERNATIONAL CALLS

International calls can be made from just about any telephone booth in Germany. It costs only €.13 per minute to call the United States, day or night, no matter how long the call lasts. Use a phone card. If you don't have a good deal with a calling card, there are many stores that offer international calls at rates well below that which you will pay from a phone booth. At a hotel, rates will be at least double the regular charge, so **avoid making international calls from your room.**

LOCAL CALLS

A local call from a telephone booth costs €.10 per minute. You can drop the local area code.

LONG-DISTANCE CALLS

Dial the zero before the area code when making a long-distance call within Germany.

LONG-DISTANCE SERVICES

AT&T, MCI, and Sprint access codes make calling long distance relatively convenient, but you may find the local access number blocked in many hotel rooms. First ask the hotel operator to connect you. If the hotel operator balks, ask for an international operator, or dial the international operator yourself. One way to improve your odds of getting connected to your long-distance carrier is to travel with more than one company's calling card (a hotel may block Sprint, for example, but not MCI). If all else fails, call from a pay phone.

►**ACCESS CODES: AT&T Direct** (tel. 0800/225–5288). **MCI WorldPhone** (tel. 0800/888–8000). **Sprint International Access** (tel. 0800/888–0013).

MOBILE PHONES

The standard mobile phones used in the United States and Canada are not compatible with Germany's GSM digital cellphone network. Because public phones are not nearly as ubiquitous as in North America, you should seriously consider renting a GSM cellphone if you intend to make calls regularly. At Munich's airport the V2 Connect shop rents cellphones.

►**PHONE RENTALS: V2 Connect** (tel. 089/973–5110).

PHONE CARDS

A phone card is a must if you think you'll be using public phones. You can purchase one, among other places, at post offices, newsstands, and exchange places. Most phone booths have instructions in English as well as German. Another advantage of the card: it charges only what the call costs. Coin-operated phones, which take €0.10, €0.20, €0.50, €1, and €2 coins, don't make change. Unfortunately telephone booths are not a common feature on the streets, so be prepared to ask locals where to find one.

Time

Germany is on Central European Time, which is six hours ahead of Eastern Standard Time and nine hours ahead of Pacific Standard Time. Germans use military time (1 PM is indicated as 13:00) and write the date before the month, so October 3 will appear as 03.10.

Tipping

The service charges on bills is sufficient for most tips in your hotel, though you should **tip bellhops and porters**; €1 per bag or service is ample. It's also customary to leave a small tip (a euro or so per night) for the room-cleaning staff. Whether you tip the desk clerk depends on whether he or she has given you any special service.

Service charges are included in all restaurant checks (listed as *Bedienung*), as is tax (listed as *MWST*). Nonetheless, it is customary to **round up the bill to the nearest euro or to leave about 5%** (give it to the waiter or waitress as you pay the bill, don't leave it on the table, as that's considered rude). Bartenders and servers also expect a 2%–5% tip.

In taxis **round up the fare about a euro** as a tip. Only give more if you have particularly cumbersome or heavy luggage.

Tours

For the cheapest sightseeing tour of the city center on wheels, board Streetcar 19 outside the Hauptbahnhof on Bahnhofplatz and make the 15-minute journey to Max Weber Platz. Explore the streets around the square, part of the old Bohemian residential area of Haidhausen (with some of the city's best bars and restaurants, many on the villagelike Kirchenstrasse), and then return by a different route on Streetcar 18 to Karlsplatz. A novel way of seeing the city is to hop on one of the bike-rickshaws. The bike-powered two-seater cabs operate between

Marienplatz and the Chinesischer Turm in the Englischer Garten. Just hail one—or book ahead by calling.

City Hopper Touren offers daily escorted bike tours March–October. Bookings must be made in advance, and starting times are negotiable. Radius Touristik has bicycle tours from May through the beginning of October at 10:15 and 2; the cost, including bike rental, is €7.70. Mike's Bike Tours is run by a young American who hires German students to take visitors on a two- to three-hour spin through Munich. The tours start daily at the Old Town Hall, the Altes Rathaus, at 11:20 and 3:50. They cost €14, including bike rental.

➤**FEES AND SCHEDULES: Bike-rickshaws** (tel. 089/129–4808). **City Hopper Touren** (tel. 089/272–1131). **Mike's Bike Tours** (tel. 089/651–4275). **Radius Touristik** (Arnulfstr. 3, opposite Platforms 30–36 in the Hauptbahnhof, Leopoldvorstadt, tel. 089/596–113).

BUS TOURS

Bus excursions to the Alps, to Austria, to the royal palaces and castles of Bavaria, or along the Romantic Road can be booked through DER. Next to the main train station, Panorama Tours operates numerous trips, including the Royal Castles Tour (Schlösserfahrt) of "Mad" King Ludwig's dream palaces; the cost is €41, excluding entrance fees to the palaces. Bookings for both companies can also be made through all major hotels in the city. The tours depart from in front of the Hauptbahnhof outside the Hertie department store.

A variety of city bus tours is offered by Panorama Tours. The blue buses operate year-round, departing from in front of the Hertie department store on Bahnhofplatz. A one-hour tour of Munich highlights leaves daily at 10, 11, 11:30, noon, 1, 2:30, 3, and 4. The cost is €11. A 2½-hour city tour departs daily at 10 AM and includes brief visits to the Alte Pinakothek, the Peterskirche, and Marienplatz for the glockenspiel. An afternoon tour, also 2½ hours and starting at 2:30 PM, includes a tour of Schloss Nymphenburg. The cost of each tour is €19. Another 2½-hour tour, departing Saturday, Sunday, and Monday at 10 AM, includes a visit to the Bavaria film studios. The cost is €23. A four-hour tour, starting daily at 10 AM and 2:30 PM includes a visit to the Olympic Park. The cost is €19. The München bei Nacht tour provides 4½ hours of Munich by night and includes dinner and a show at the Hofbräuhaus, a trip up the Olympic Tower to admire the lights of the city, and a final drink in a nightclub. It departs April through November, Friday and Saturday at 7:30 PM; the cost is €60.

Yellow Cab Stadtrundfahrten has a fleet of yellow double-decker buses, in which tours are offered simultaneously in eight languages. They leave hourly between 10 AM and 4 PM from in front of the Elisenhof shopping complex on Bahnhofsplatz.

➤FEES AND SCHEDULES: DER (Hauptbahnhofpl. 2, in the main train station building, Leopoldvorstadt, tel. 089/5514–0100). **Panorama Tours** (Arnulfstr. 8, Leopoldvorstadt, tel. 089/5490–7560). **Yellow Cab Stadtrundfahrten** (Sendlinger-Tor-Pl. 2, Isarvorstadt, tel. 089/303–631).

WALKING TOURS
Downtown Munich is only a mile square and is easily explored on foot. Almost all the major attractions in the city center are on the interlinking web of pedestrian streets that run from Karlsplatz, by the main train station, to Marienplatz and the Viktualienmarkt and extend north around the Frauenkirche and up to Odeonsplatz. The two tourist information offices issue a free map with suggested walking tours.

Two-hour tours of the old city center are given daily in summer (March–October) and on Friday and Saturday in winter (November–February). Tours organized by the visitor center start at 10:30 and 1 in the center of Marienplatz. The cost is €8. Munich Walks conducts daily tours of the old city and sites related to the

Third Reich era. The cost is €10. Tours depart daily from the Hauptbahnhof, outside the EurAide office by Track 11, and also pick up latecomers outside the McDonalds at Karlsplatz.

►**FEES AND SCHEDULES: The Original Munich Walks** (tel. 089/5502–9374, www.radius–munich.com).

Train Travel

The Hauptbahnhof handles all long-distance rail services; trains to and from some destinations in Bavaria use the adjoining Starnbergerbahnhof, which is under the same roof. The high-speed InterCity Express (ICE) trains connect Munich, Augsburg, Frankfurt, and Hamburg on one line; Munich, Nuremberg, Würzburg, and Hamburg on another. Call for information on train schedules; most railroad information staff speak English. For tickets and travel information, go to the station information office or try the ABR-DER travel agency, right by the station on Bahnhofplatz.

►**TRAIN INFORMATION: ABR-DER** (Bahnhofpl., Leopold-vorstadt, tel. 089/551–40200). **Hauptbahnhof** (Bahnhofpl., Leopoldvorstadt, tel. 089/2333–0256 or 089/2333–0257; 01805/996–633 for train schedules).

Transportation around Munich

Munich has an efficient and well-integrated public transportation system, consisting of the U-bahn (subway), the S-bahn (suburban railway), the Strassenbahn (streetcars), and buses. Marienplatz forms the heart of the U-bahn and S-bahn network, which operates from around 5 AM to 1 AM. An all-night tram and bus service operates on main routes within the city. For a clear explanation in English of how the system works, pick up a copy of *Rendezvous mit München*, available free of charge at all tourist offices.

Fares are uniform for the entire system. As long as you are traveling in the same direction, you can transfer from one mode of transportation to another on the same ticket. You can also interrupt your journey as often as you like, and time-punched tickets are valid for up to four hours, depending on the number of zones you travel through. Fares are constantly creeping upward, but a basic *Einzelfahrkarte* (one-way ticket) costs €2 for a ride in the inner zone and €1 for a short journey of up to four stops. If you're taking a number of trips around the city, save money by buying a *Mehrfahrtenkarte*, or multiple strip ticket. Red strip tickets are valid for children under 15 only. Blue strips cover adults—€9 buys a 10-strip ticket. All but the shortest inner-area journeys (up to four stops) cost two strips (one for young people between 15 and 21), which must be validated at one of the many time-punching machines at stations or on buses and trams. For two to five people on a short stay the best option is the *Partner-Tageskarte* ticket, which provides unlimited travel (maximum of two adults, plus three children under 15). It is valid weekdays from 9 AM to 6 AM the following day and at any time on weekends. The costs are €7.50 for an inner-zone ticket and €15 for the entire network. The day card exists in single version for €4.50 for the inner city, €9 for the whole network. A three-day card is also available, costing €11 for a single and €17.50 in the partner version.

The *Welcome Card* covers transport within the city boundaries and includes up to 50% reductions in admission to many museums and attractions. The card, obtainable from visitor information offices, costs €6.50 for one day and €15.50 for three days. A three-day card for two people costs €22.50.

All tickets are sold at the blue dispensers at U- and S-bahn stations and at some bus and streetcar stops. Bus drivers have single tickets (the most expensive kind). There are ticket vending machines in trams, but they don't offer the strip cards. Otherwise tourist offices and Mehrfahrtenkarten booths (which display a white K on a green background) also sell tickets. Spot checks are common and carry an automatic fine of €30 if you're caught without a valid ticket. Holders of a EurailPass, a Youth Pass, or an Inter-Rail card can travel free on all suburban railway trains the (S-Bahn).

Travel Agencies

DER, the official German travel agency, has outlets all over Munich. The two most central ones are in the main railway station building and at the Münchner-Freiheit Square, in Schwabing.

➤CONTACTS: **American Express** (Promenadenpl. 6, City Center, tel. 089/290–900). **DER** (Bahnhofpl. 2, Leopoldvorstadt, tel. 089/5514–0100; Münchner-Freiheit 6, Schwabing, tel. 089/336–033).

Visitor Information

The Hauptbahnhof tourist office is open Monday–Saturday 9–8 and Sunday 10–6; the Info-Service in the Rathaus is open weekdays 10–8 and Saturday 10–4.

For information on the Bavarian mountain region south of Munich, contact the Tourismusverband München-Oberbayern.

➤TOURIST INFORMATION: **Hauptbahnhof** (Bahnhofpl. 2, next to DER travel agency, Leopoldvorstadt, tel. 089/2333–0123, www.munich-tourist.de). **Info-Service** (Marienpl., City Center, tel. 089/2332–8242). **Tourismusverband München-Oberbayern** (Upper Bavarian Regional Tourist Office; Bodenseestr. 113, Pasing D–81243, tel. 089/829–180).

Web Sites

Do check out the World Wide Web when planning your trip. You'll find everything from weather forecasts to virtual tours of famous cities. Be sure to **visit Fodors.com** (www.fodors.com), a complete travel-planning site. You can research prices and book plane tickets, hotel rooms, rental cars, vacation packages, and more. In addition, you can post your pressing questions in the Travel Talk section. Other planning tools include a currency converter and weather reports, and there are loads of links to travel resources. One site that goes in-depth regarding international telephone systems and modem hook-up trouble-shooting is www.kropla.com.

Many German tourism-related Web sites have an English-language version, usually indicated by an icon of the American or British flag. For general information on Germany, visit www.visits-to-germany.com, the German National Tourist Office's site.

Weather

The following are the average daily maximum and minimum temperatures for Munich.

MUNICH

Jan.	35F	1C	May	64F	18C	Sept.	67F	20C
	23	− 5		45	7		48	9
Feb.	38F	3C	June	70F	21C	Oct.	56F	14C
	23	− 5		51	11		40	4
Mar.	48F	9C	July	74F	23C	Nov.	44F	7C
	30	− 1		55	13		33	0
Apr.	56F	14C	Aug.	73F	23C	Dec.	36F	2C
	38	3		54	12		26	− 4

index

Fodor's
Key to the Guides

America's guidebook leader publishes guides for every kind of traveler. Check out our many series and find your perfect match.

Fodor's Gold Guides

America's favorite travel-guide series offers the most detailed insider reviews of hotels, restaurants, and attractions in all price ranges, plus great background information, smart tips, and useful maps.

Fodor's Road Guide USA

Big guides for a big country—the most comprehensive guides to America's roads, packed with places to stay, eat, and play across the U.S.A. Just right for road warriors, family vacationers, and cross-country trekkers.

COMPASS AMERICAN GUIDES

Stunning guides from top local writers and photographers, with gorgeous photos, literary excerpts, and colorful anecdotes. A must-have for culture mavens, history buffs, and new residents.

Fodor's CITYPACKS

Concise city coverage with a foldout map. The right choice for urban travelers who want everything under one cover.

Fodor's EXPLORING GUIDES

Hundreds of color photos bring your destination to life. Lively stories lend insight into the culture, history, and people.

Fodor's POCKET GUIDES

For travelers who need only the essentials. The best of Fodor's in pocket-size packages for just $9.95.

Fodor's To Go
Credit-card–size, magnetized color microguides that fit in the palm of your hand—perfect for "stealth" travelers or as gifts.

Fodor's FLASHMAPS
Every resident's map guide. 60 easy-to-follow maps of public transit, parks, museums, zip codes, and more.

Fodor's CITYGUIDES
Sourcebooks for living in the city: Thousands of in-the-know listings for restaurants, shops, sports, nightlife, and other city resources.

Fodor's *AROUND THE CITY WITH KIDS*
68 great ideas for family days, recommended by resident parents. Perfect for exploring in your own backyard or on the road.

Fodor's ESCAPES
Fill your trip with once-in-a-lifetime experiences, from ballooning in Chianti to overnighting in the Moroccan desert. These full color dream books point the way.

Fodor's FYI
Get tips from the pros on planning the perfect trip. Learn how to pack, fly hassle-free, plan a honeymoon or cruise, stay healthy on the road, and travel with your baby.

Fodor's Languages for Travelers
Practice the local language before hitting the road. Available in phrase books, cassette sets, and CD sets.

Karen Brown's Guides
Engaging guides to the most charming inns and B&Bs in the U.S.A. and Europe, with easy-to-follow inn-to-inn itineraries.

Baedeker's Guides
Comprehensive guides, trusted since 1829, packed with A–Z reviews and star ratings.

FODOR'S POCKET MUNICH

EDITOR: Christina Knight

Editorial Contributors: Marton Radai, Ted Shoemaker

Editorial Production: Kristin Milavec

Maps: David Lindroth, *cartographer*; Bob Blake and Rebecca Baer, *map editors*

Design: Fabrizio La Rocca, *creative director*; Tigist Getachew, *art director*; Jolie Novak, *senior picture editor*; Melanie Marin, *photo editor*

Production/Manufacturing: Bob Shields

Cover Photo (Hypobank, Munich): Hubert Stadler/Corbis

IMPORTANT TIP

Although all prices, opening times, and other details in this book are based on information supplied to us at press time, changes occur all the time in the travel world, and Fodor's cannot accept responsibility for facts that become outdated or for inadvertent errors or omissions. So **always confirm information when it matters**, especially if you're making a detour to visit a specific place.

SPECIAL SALES

Fodor's Travel Publications are available at special discounts for bulk purchases for sales promotions or premiums. Special editions, including personalized covers, excerpts of existing guides, and corporate imprints, can be created in large quantities for special needs. For more information, contact your local bookseller or write to Special Markets, Fodor's Travel Publications, 1745 Broadway, New York, New York 10019. Inquiries from Canada should be directed to your local Canadian bookseller or sent to Random House of Canada, Ltd., Marketing Department, 2775 Matheson Boulevard East, Mississauga, Ontario L4W 4P7. Inquiries from the United Kingdom should be sent to Fodor's Travel Publications, 20 Vauxhall Bridge Road, London SW1V 2SA, England.

PRINTED IN THE UNITED STATES OF AMERICA

10 9 8 7 6 5 4 3 2 1